YOU CAN BANK
ON YOUR VOICE

YOU CAN BANK ON YOUR VOICE

Your Guide to a Successful Career in Voice-Overs

RODNEY SAULSBERRY

Published by Tomdor Publishing, LLC
P.O. Box 1735, Agoura Hills, CA 91376-1735
Tel: 818-207-2682 Fax: 818-707-8591
www.tomdorpublishing.com

PUBLISHER'S CATALOGING-IN-PUBLICATION DATA
Saulsberry, Rodney.
   You can bank on your voice: your guide to a successful career in voice-overs / Rodney Saulsberry — Agoura Hills, Calif. : Tomdor Publishing, 2004.
       p.   cm.
       Includes bibliographical references and index.
       ISBN 0-9747678-0-8
       SAN: 255-8319

       Library of Congress Control Number: 2003099036

       1. Voice-overs. 2. Television announcing—Vocational guidance. 3. Radio announcing—Vocational guidance. 4. Voice in motion pictures. 5. Acting—Vocational guidance. 6. Television advertising—Vocational guidance. 7. Radio advertising—Vocational guidance. 8. Voice culture. I. Title.

PN1992.8.A6 S28 2004
791.45/028/023—dc22   CIP

Printed in the United States of America

10 9 8 7 6 5 4

Cover design by Kristine Mills-Knoble
Text design and layout by Mary Jo Zazueta
Back cover photography by Carrie Cavalier

This book is dedicated to my wife, Helen, and my daughter, Traci. I could not have done this without the two of you. I love you.

Also to my parents, Thomas and Dorothy Saulsberry, you made me the man that I am today. I love you.

Contents

CHAPTER 1   First Things First 23

What Is a Voice-Over?
How to Get Started
Choosing a Voice-Over Instructor
The Voice-Over Demo
Go West, Young Man, Go West

CHAPTER 2   Getting a Foot in the Door 37

Joining the Unions
Non-Union vs. Union Work
Finding an Agent
The Agency House Reel
The Audition
What Casting Directors Expect from You, the Actor
My First Voice-Over Agency

CHAPTER 3   The Session 61

Interpreting Your Copy
In Review
Commercial Sessions
Trailer Sessions
Promo Sessions
Animation Sessions
Demos
Scratch Tracks
Tags
Legal Tags
My Trailer Love Affair

Through hard work, enormous talent, and perseverance, my good friend, Rodney Saulsberry has risen up the Hollywood ladder to become one of the top voice-over artists in the industry. He does it all and does it well. He makes a huge bundle of dough doing it, too. As a young man, he's right at the height of his abilities and popularity; however, now he wants to share his knowledge, his techniques and his secrets with all of you. I know he'd like me to think of this as a sign of his generosity and maturity, but I can't. I view it as total insanity.

Don't get me wrong. Nobody could be more qualified to write this book than Rodney. In fact, I can't think of a more appropriate teacher in the highly specialized field of voice-overs. As a cartoon voice on my *Spider-Man* animated series for Fox TV, Rodney frequently took the words I'd written and made them sing (for the Marvel Comics purists among you, Rodney portrayed the character "Joe Robbie Robertson"). His ability to interpret copy would make any writer proud. That's why he's considered the best.

Any producer who needs to create a spot to sell a product, give voice to a cartoon character, or add spoken words to a promo or movie trailer literally has millions of dollars riding on the ability of the voice-over artist to perform these important tasks. Under these tight circumstances, the skill, talent, and professionalism of the actor is very important. Producers and studios pay top dollar for good voice-over talent. Time is money, and they want to trust that their time will not be wasted, so they only seek out the best people for the job.

Making you one of the best is the prime objective of this authoritative book. You are literally holding in your hands the key to a lucrative future in a very important profession.

But it's madness to hand over the keys to the treasure chest like this. Sheer madness! Surely Rodney's gripped in some sort of temporary insanity, one from which he's undoubtedly bound to recover. You should count yourself lucky that you've picked up this book before Rodney comes to his senses and recalls all copies of it. Until then, don't tell too many people about the gold mine you're holding in your hands.

And don't hold your breath waiting for me to write a book teaching anyone how to be a successful producer/writer for children's television. It ain't gonna happen.

John Semper, Jr., Producer/Writer
Spider-Man and *Static Shock*

The fact that you picked up this book is a good sign that you're interested in voice-overs. Maybe you know someone who does them for a living, or maybe you're looking for a new vocation. Perhaps you've just always dreamed of one day breaking into this exciting industry. Whatever your reason, this book, *You Can Bank on Your Voice*, will help you get started, and hopefully enjoy a long, successful, money-driven career.

When I decided to write a book on this subject, I wanted to create something that I would find beneficial if I were trying to break into the voice-over industry. I also wanted to appeal to the experienced voice-over artists by writing about advanced techniques that could help them sharpen their skills and make them better.

I share my own personal experiences because I believe it gives the book a degree of honesty and credibility. From the sample copy and vocal exercises in the appendixes, to the casting and voice-over training contacts in the resource section, I have tried to provide you with some of the many tools you'll need to be successful.

Not only do you receive the benefits of my knowledge, but I've gathered contributions from some of the best voice-over instructors and casting directors in the business and added them to this book.

This is your chance to learn about an occupation that will let you set your own hours; meet other talented and exciting people; travel to great studios for work; or, with today's advanced digital technology, stay in the comfort of your own home, and make a fortune. You make the choice.

It doesn't matter where you live—voice-over work is available anywhere in the country and throughout the world. Your age is not a factor. Advertisers are looking for real people and real voices with the passion and talent to turn their products into something consumers must have and can't do without.

Today there are more professional outlets for the human voice than ever before. You could not have picked a better time to be interested in the lucrative field of voice-overs. I hope you come away from the experience of reading my book with a better understanding of this unique profession. Let's get started on your road to voice-over riches.

ACKNOWLEDGMENTS

I gratefully acknowledge my entire family, all of my friends and everyone who contributed to the making of this book. I sincerely love and thank you all.

YOU CAN BANK
ON YOUR VOICE

A Day in the Life of a Voice-Over Artist

I'm up this sunny Tuesday at 7:00 A.M. I wash my face, brush my teeth, and go downstairs to the kitchen to fix myself a cup of green tea. I pop last night's leftovers into the microwave and sit down at the kitchen table to nibble a bit. It takes a little food to clear my raspy throat in the morning and soothe my vocal cords.

As I read the morning paper, my fax machine starts to hum, probably with voice-over scripts for my first session. I've got my first session at 7:30, in my home studio, which I affectionately call the Money Box. A poster of golfing phenom Tiger Woods adorns its door. I put his picture there because he's a hard worker, he's a winner and he makes a lot of money.

This morning, through the wonders of technology, I am working simultaneously with an engineer in North Carolina, the client in Nashville and another voice-over talent in Chicago. We work for a grand total of fifteen minutes on a sixty-second in-store spot for Cingular Wireless.

My second session is scheduled to start at eight. I've got just enough time to go back into the kitchen, fix myself another cup of tea, say good morning to my wife, good-bye to my teenage daughter as she rushes off to school, get my next script from the fax machine, and sit down for a second to study it.

At eight, hooked up to an engineer and client in New Orleans, I'm at the microphone joyously delivering copy about the great taste of Zatarain's Dirty Rice. My third session isn't until nine. Back in the kitchen, my wife and I are talking about what her day entails. At nine sharp, armed with my scripts and reading glasses in hand, I saunter back into the studio to extol the wonderful virtues of Clippers Basketball for KTLA Television in Los Angeles before hitting the shower at 9:35.

I pull out of the driveway of my spacious suburban home, and I'm stopped by one of my neighbors who lets me know how much he likes my new Mercedes. Turning out of the cul-de-sac I reflect on how grateful I am to

God for blessing me with a wonderful, healthy family, and for making it possible for us to live in this beautiful neighborhood with its highly regarded school system— all because of a successful voice-over career.

It's a normal day on the 101 freeway—crowded. After listening to some good music on my favorite FM radio station, I switch to an AM station to listen to talk radio. The closer I get to my next session at LA Studios, the more I think about warming up my voice. I do this every day by searching the dial and repeating aloud everything I hear on the radio—the Dow Jones report, the weather, sports, traffic, and the entertainment news. At the end of each segment I'll replace the reporter's name with my own: "I'm Rodney Saulsberry and you're listening to KNX 1070 news radio."

I can be very animated. I've had people in carpools on the freeway looking into my car and wondering if I'm some kind of nut. By speaking in rhythmic cadences, I exercise my tongue and improve my flexibility.

Suddenly, I stop talking and switching stations because I hear my own voice on a commercial. I don't repeat these words; I just listen. Although I've listened to my voice countless times on the radio and on television, hearing it never gets old and always stops me cold. Finally I switch to an FM station, and there I am again on another spot. Now I'm totally hyped and eternally grateful.

It's 10:45 A.M. when I pull into the lot of LA Studios. The parking attendant takes my car and I walk into the studio for my 11:00 A.M. session, a Toyota Camry television commercial. I'm really excited about this because I did the 2003 Camry spot, which has brought me a lot of money in residuals, and today I'm working on the 2004 ad for the Burrell Advertising Agency in Chicago. If this campaign does half as well as the 2003 one, I will be a very happy man.

After I finish, I head over to the William Morris Agency in Beverly Hills to read some audition scripts and have a brief meeting with my voice-over agent. He informs me that a booking just came in from New Line Cinema. They want me to do some trailers for the movie *Dumb & Dumberer* at a studio in West Hollywood called Point 360 Woodholly at 4:00 P.M.

At 2:15, I'm enjoying a late lunch at one of my favorite eateries, Chin Chins, on Sunset Boulevard. I have one of my favorite dishes, chicken fried rice. At 3:45, I pull into the parking lot at Point 360 Woodholly studios.

Twenty minutes later, I'm back in an environment I know all too well—traffic. Rush hour is wicked. I'm moving at a snail's pace, and I haven't even gotten on the freeway yet. Sometimes, on days like this, I'll go over to the Farmers Market on Third and Fairfax or the Four Seasons Hotel on Doheny Drive to have a glass of red wine, chill and let the traffic die down. Today I'm just cruising and talking on my cell phone to one of my buddies when my pager goes off.

It's my agent. We talk about the next day's schedule, which includes some animation work on a cartoon series called *Static Shock* for Warner Brothers.

As my family and I are finishing up dinner a little after six, my agent pages me again. On the phone, we discuss what time New Line Cinema is going to dial me up on my digital telephone line at home later to record some extra lines for the *Dumb & Dumberer* trailer session I did earlier.

A man's work is never done, so back to the Money Box I go. It's amazing what I have accomplished in this little room. Perhaps I should call it the Little Room That Could.

At midnight, my wife is sound asleep. I lie next to her, our bedroom darkness sliced by the flickering TV image of Jay Leno on the *Tonight Show*. I gaze at the screen, ponder Jay's corny bit, and think, *Damn I'm lucky!*

First Things First

J ust like in any other new endeavor you tackle, there's a beginning process that takes you to the middle and hopefully ends with your desired goal attained. In this chapter, I want to supply you with important information and key definitions that will make the rest of your read easier. We'll discuss what it takes to get started and who can help you do it. There are exercises here that you can do at home and on your current job to prepare for your voice-over career. This is the foundation segment of the book. Let's start with this basic instruction, and remember to have fun.

What Is a Voice-Over?

A voice-over is a narration or comment off camera, promoting a message about a person, place, or thing for commercial purposes. When I say "The stylish 2003 Toyota Camry, it speaks for itself" in the middle of a car commercial, that's a voice-over. At the end of all my Zatarain's TV spots I say, "Jazz it up with Zatarain's," that's a voice-over. And when I tell you that a certain movie "Starts Friday at a theater near you" in a movie trailer, you've just heard another voice-over. You hear me but you don't see me.

Voice-overs are also heard in industrial films, documentaries, and animation. When you log onto AOL (America Online) and you hear "Welcome, you've got mail," that's a voice-over. Audiobooks, infomercials, and CD-ROMs are all part of what constitutes voice-overs. In a nutshell, a voice-over is anything that has to do with vocal presentation through a media outlet.

How to Get Started

The first thing you can do before you spend a dime to pursue your new career is to follow this three-week program designed to let you hear your voice, so you can decide if you want to go any farther. When you speak normally, you don't listen to yourself, so you don't know and are not aware of how you sound. It's important to know how you'll sound saying the words that we all hear in commercials every day.

⭘ During the first week, read sections of the newspaper out loud every day. Find a paragraph of the sports section and try to imitate a sportscaster. Also read the business and entertainment sections. Be a movie critic by reading the movie reviews out loud.

○ Second week: Pull out some canned or boxed food and read everything that's written on it. Cereal boxes tend to have great advertising copy. Read the copy faster and slower out loud. Try it with a happy voice, then a sad voice. Repeat this process for at least fifteen minutes every day. While you're out, read the advertisements on the sides of buses and backs of trucks and billboards. This can also be done during commutes for people who take the train.

○ By the third week you should know if you like the sound of your voice. Now you need to know if anybody else does. Find an impartial family member or friend to listen to you read the newspaper and some of the other things you practiced in week two. If they don't cringe and leave the room or ask you to get out, this is an indication that you may have a voice that is at least pleasant to the ear.

Now it's time to spend a little money. Invest in a small cassette tape recorder. Read more ad copy from magazines and record yourself over and over. Use different copy each time and don't become too familiar with any one piece. Don't memorize; keep it fresh by doing it a new way each time. Place emphasis on different words, vary your pauses. Listen to yourself. Determine your vocal capabilities. Ask yourself, *Is my voice high or low? Am I better at reading faster or slower? Is my voice normal or quirky (peculiar)?* If you have difficulty pronouncing certain words, work on them.

Don't be discouraged if your voice is quirky. You might be perfect for animation.

Turn on the radio when you're at home or in your car. Watch television commercials every chance you get. Listen to the way people talk in those ads. Become observant with your ears and be critical of the things you hear. If you own a VCR, record about two hours of programming. Review the tape later and write down the copy from your favorite spots and read them out loud.

It's not enough just to have a good voice; you have to know how to use it. You have to learn how to read and interpret copy. The best place to learn these things is in a weekly voice-over class. If your time is limited, maybe you can attend a weekend seminar. Online seminars are also an option. Check your local actors union for information on voice-over classes in animation, commercials, and promos.

In Los Angeles you can find listings of vocal coaches in *The Voice-Over Research Guide*. Other magazines that will help you get information about commercial production, casting, and ad agencies include *Ad Week*, *Variety*, *Animation Magazine*, and the *Hollywood Reporter*.

For the absolute best in informational and educational online voice-over websites, I highly recommend *www.LA411.com* or *www.NewYork411.com*, and the Great Voice Company at *www.greatvoice.com*. Be sure to research the resource section of this book where you will find an extensive list of voice-over agencies from around the country. Hopefully you will find a few listings from your town.

If you're serious and you really want to be in this business, you have to learn the craft. Acting classes can help you when it comes to conveying emotion and personality in your commercial reads. I'm a big fan of doing everything you can to get better. I would also recommend taking singing lessons to learn proper breathing and interpretation techniques. Being a singer sure didn't hurt me. If you want the chance to get all that the voice-over business has to offer, you have to put in the work. Voice-over is not a side job unless you only want to make side money. Not everyone is going to be successful, but at least give it an honest try by doing everything it takes to be the best you can be.

Concentrate on getting yourself into a voice-over class. Let's talk about how to make sure the vocal instructor you choose is the right one for you.

Choosing a Voice-Over Instructor

Word of mouth and referrals are two ways to find a voice-over teacher. If you have friends in the business who carry on and on about how good an instructor is, that would be a great place to start.

Perhaps you don't realize how much our society is influenced by word of mouth. Think about it: It's Saturday afternoon and you're starting to think about what you're going to do later that evening. Finally, you decide to take in a movie. When you open up the entertainment section of the newspaper you take a look at the listings and a light goes off in your head. You spot the film your best friend and your cousin told you was a "must see." Decision made, you go to see it. Word of mouth influenced your decision. You heard the movie was good from a couple of people, so you went to see it.

You woke up with a stiff neck and you haven't been able to turn your head to the right in two days. Your mother's beautician's son is a chiropractor who according to your mom is the best! When you fill out your medical questionnaire on your first visit to his office, you note who referred you. An hour later, the success of that referral has you spinning your head around with the flexibility of an owl.

Once you've gotten the name of an instructor, arrange a free consultation with him. Just because he is good for your friend, doesn't mean he's the perfect coach for you. When you arrange the consultation and tour of the teaching facility, there are some important things about which you should inquire:

○ **What is my financial commitment?** You shouldn't pay more than $600 for six to twelve lessons.

○ **Do I have to pay everything up front?** Many instructors will want the full sum while others will have you pay as you go. If you miss a week, you don't pay.

○ **How many students per class?** There should be no more than twelve students in your class to ensure individual attention. You want to make sure that you get quality time at the microphone. You can't be good at the mic if you don't constantly work with it.

○ **Do you have a state-of-the-art digital production studio?** The studio should be equipped with a voice-over booth for the actor to record in isolation and the ability to put your practice performances onto a CD that you can take home. You also want to make sure that in two hours you get at least three times on the microphone.

○ **Do I have to bring broadcast copy?** Some students want to bring their own copy to class. A good instructor will supply professional broadcast material at every lesson. It should focus on whatever the class curriculum is (i.e., commercial, promo, animation, audiobooks, etc.).

○ **What should I expect after my sessions?** Your instructor should be able to articulate what you're supposed to get out of the course. During your free consultation—before you spend any money —you should discuss what your goals are and how the instructor can help you reach them.

○ **Is this a beginner's class?** Will the other students be more or less experienced than you? Find out the women to men ratio. You don't want to be in a class with all women or all men. It's nice to have a good mix.

You might also consider private instruction. A one- or two-hour private lesson will definitely give you all the individual attention you need. Private lessons cost between $30 and $50 per hour and from $100 to $150 for two hours.

Successful experienced voice-over artists like myself who teach are in high demand for coaching. Our time is limited because of our busy schedules, but when we commit to a two- to three-hour seminar session, the class fills up quickly. Newcomers are very interested in learning from professionals who are still active on the battlefield.

Casting directors who teach are good voice-over instructors because they know what casting directors are looking for. As a student in a casting director's class, you have the opportunity to impress him with your skills, which might lead to an audition for a commercial he is casting.

If you can't find a voice-over class in your town, look for an acting or improvisation class. Good instruction early on in your voice-over career will help you build a solid foundation for your future.

Next step: After your lessons, if you think you need more instruction, take another class. If you think you're ready, now it's time to make your first voice-over demo.

If you live in San Francisco, Seattle, Los Angeles, San Diego, or New York, you can take voice-over classes at the Learning Annex in your area. You can call or check their website at www.learningannex.com **for schedules.**

THE VOICE-OVER DEMO

Once you've made the decision to record a demo tape, which I believe is the most important tool in your voice-over arsenal, the next step is to find someone to help you put it together. That person could be a voice-over teacher, director, or engineer.

You should start with a consultation. You and the person working with you have to discuss what your content will be. If this is a commercial demo, you must gather ad copy to read. This also applies to trailer, animation, narration, and promo demos.

The consultation gives you a chance to express some

of your interests. Talk about current television and radio commercials. What do they mean to you? What appeals to you? What products would you like to promote on your first demo? Sometimes we perform better if we like, believe, and relate to a product.

Don't put anything on your demo you can't reproduce vocally in person.

I am not a lawyer nor am I familiar with copyright infringement laws, but generally if this is your first demo and you don't have any authentic samples of past work, you'll have to make up product names, or use known brands in your presentations at your own risk. The first demo I recorded before I got an agent consisted of five fake commercial samples using well-known products. I never had a problem, and I have never heard of any of my contemporaries getting into any trouble for the same practice. If you take the latter route, be sure to use the final product for demo purposes only, and do not use it for commercial broadcast.

Versatility is another consideration. You want to choose enough different types of copy to show your range. You should not have back-to-back car commercials on your demo or consecutive food ads. Try to mix things up a bit. Vary your vocal pitch if you have that ability. Give the listener a taste of your lower, mid, and higher ranges. Don't be vocally versatile just for the sake of it if you don't have ranges in your voice. If you do one thing and that's all you have to offer, that's okay. Put your best foot forward.

After you record your spots the editing process should be addressed. You want to grab your listener's attention at the very beginning of your demo and never let their attention span wane away from your presentation. Be sure to have what you think are your best spots at the beginning.

Pacing is important. Make sure the presentation is moving at a rapid pace, even when you are speaking slowly. Separation from spot to spot should be clear, and all transitions should be smooth.

Your commercial demo, in my opinion, should be no longer than two minutes. In fact, one minute and fifty seconds of a fast-paced demonstration with four to five snippets of different spots should be just enough for the listener to get an idea of your vocal capabilities.

The cost of getting a high-quality produced demo can be expensive. A state-of-the-art digitally equipped studio can cost in the range of $65 to $125 an hour. It shouldn't take you any more than six to eight hours to complete. Editing and mixing could make it a slightly longer process. You can cut down on your recording time by making the demo when you are truly ready to do so. Once you have taken a few voice-over classes and spent some quality time in front of the microphone, you'll be able to read copy quickly and precisely, which will cut down on your takes (recorded attempts) and get you out of the recording booth quicker, which will in turn save you time and money. Make sure that the studio you choose is a place that is accustomed to producing voice-over demos. The studio that recorded your brother's punk rock band is not necessarily the right place for you. Ask a representative from the studio to let you hear some samples of the work they've done with other voice talent.

When you're completely satisfied with your demo, find a place to get duplicate CDs or cassette copies made. The same place that recorded your demo will probably know of a few duplication houses, or you can search the Internet. This is the least expensive part of the process. In the beginning, I would not recommend getting any more than thirty-five to fifty CDs, especially if you don't have an agent. Your agent may want you to add or delete something, and you'll have to go back into the studio and redo it. Keep in mind the cassette tape is still used in the industry but the CD is the more popular way to present the demo.

For the experienced voice-over artist, the demo should contain a true representation of your best and most recent work.

If you feel ready, now it's time to find an agent.

Go West, Young Man, Go West

The national touring company of the gospel musical *Your Arms Too Short to Box with God* arrived at the LAX airport at 5:00 P.M. Saturday, December 10, 1979. The three-week run at the Variety Arts Center on Flower Street in downtown Los Angeles was to be the last leg of the tour.

When our successful Los Angeles run was over, instead of boarding a plane and flying back home to Detroit, I decided to stay in Hollywood to fulfill my television acting and recording star dreams.

In February 1980, I got my first television acting job when I went on an audition for *Happy Days* at Paramount Studios. When I finished the audition I decided to walk around the lot for a while. I wandered onto the stage where the hit comedy *Taxi* was being filmed and found myself in the middle of a rehearsal. Tony Danza, the actor who played former boxer Tony Banta, spotted me, came over, playfully pushed me, and suggested I engage him in a playful round of slap boxing. On cue I dropped my briefcase and proceeded to do the Ali shuffle with Tony around the stage. Mid bout, Tony stopped, turned around, and said to the director, James Burrows, "Jim, this is the guy."

Jim said, "C'mon, Tony. Let's get back in the scene."

"No, I'm serious, Jim. This is the guy," Tony said.

Fifteen minutes later and after some lying about my Golden Gloves boxing experience, I was in the producer of the show, Ed Weinberger's, office signing a contract to play Carl the Boxer on *Taxi*. I am forever grateful to Tony Danza and mighty glad I didn't leave the Paramount lot after my *Happy Days* audition. I didn't get the part on *Happy Days* because they said I was too tall to play opposite the Fonz.

I went on to be a steady working actor with guest star and featured roles on *M.A.S.H.*, *The White Shadow*, *The A-Team*, *Mike Hammer*, *Dynasty*, *CHiPs*, *Falcon Crest*, *Hill Street Blues*, *Dr. Quinn Medicine Woman*, and a regular on the short-lived CBS soap opera, *Capitol*.

As a singer I recorded a couple of R&B records and enjoyed moderate success in the states as well as England. I appeared on *Soul Train* and *Dance Fever*, and my music video for the mid-tempo "Look Whatcha Done Now" played in heavy rotation on BET and VH1. I also performed on *The Lion King* and *Prince of Egypt* soundtracks.

My acting background would prove to be very valuable for things to come. As it turned out, the kid from Detroit, Michigan, whose arms were *too short to box with God*, but long enough to slap box with Tony Danza, ended up knocking out the competition with his voice.

CHAPTER 2

Getting a Foot in the Door

Y ou got your feet wet when you jumped into the introductory pages of Chapter One. In this chapter, I want to give you some insight on what it takes to get your foot in the door and make some serious money. Find out what it takes to be a union member, how to get an agent, and how to audition. You'll also get pointers from some industry heavyweights who know their stuff and are eager to help you.

JOINING THE UNIONS

There are two unions you will deal with in the voice-over business. For most television jobs you will work in the jurisdiction of the Screen Actors Guild (SAG). For radio and some television, you will work with the American Federation of Televesion and Radio Artists (AFTRA).

To become an AFTRA member, all you have to do is go to your local AFTRA office and pay an initiation fee of $1,300. You are eligible to become a SAG member after you have been an AFTRA member for one year, or if you have worked on two SAG jobs within thirty days of each other. The initiation fee to join SAG is $1,356. You will also have to pay union dues annually.

The amount you pay is based on your earnings for the year. As a union member anyone who hires you has to pay you at least a union scale fee and residuals, if warranted. The client must also contribute to the pension and welfare fund on your behalf. The unions also have retirement and health plans for which you have to reach and maintain a certain level of income yearly to be eligible. If you have a problem getting paid by an employer, the union can collect for you under the guidelines of the contract.

NON-UNION VS. UNION WORK

When you work non-union a client has the right to use your work as much as she likes without paying you any more money. Although non-union work is bigger in smaller markets and cities, you will still find your fair share of it in the larger markets, too. There usually is no contract involved. If there is a contract it will state that the one-time payment you receive is a buyout, which is generally a hefty sum due to the fact that the employer doesn't plan to pay you any residuals or monies toward your pension and welfare.

If the client is negligent and decides not to pay you or takes a long time to pay you, there is no union to help you get your money. There is no set pay scale in non-union work; your pay is negotiable.

There are agents who represent non-union talent exclusively, but they are not franchised agents. Generally, union actors are not supposed to work on non-union jobs. If your union catches you, you could be penalized monetarily or with expulsion from the union. Non-union work is great for beginners who have not joined a union yet, either because they don't have the money or they are not eligible.

FINDING AN AGENT

Once you feel you're ready for representation, get a list of the licensed voice-over agents in your area from the SAG or AFTRA unions. Make calls to find out if the agents to whom you want to submit are accepting new clients, and send your voice-over demo along with a cover letter to them. A sample letter for your use is on the following page.

Be prepared to wait at least a couple of months for a response. Most agencies have a set time that they listen to and review the many demos they receive. Some listen weekly, some bi-weekly, and some once a month.

SAMPLE AGENT SUBMISSION LETTER

Your name
Your street address
City, state, zip
E-mail
Phone number

Date

Mr. Barry Peterson
Sloan, Baker & Bauman Agency
6754 Wilshire Blvd., Suite 458
Los Angeles, CA 90036

Dear Mr. Peterson,

I am currently looking for agency representation. Enclosed please find a copy of my voice-over demo for your consideration.

I look forward to your response.

Sincerely,

Your signature

Your name typed

When you get your chance to sit down with an agent who is interested in you, conduct your own interview. Turn the tables, so to speak, and make the agent audition to represent you. You can do this by asking important questions about your concerns. Some things you may want to ask: How many agents are here? Do you get a lot of copy (audition scripts) here? How many recording booths do you have? Are you strong in trailers and promos? Do you have an animation department?

Who knows, you might not want to be with this agency after you get the answers, and they may not want you either after the meeting. You should never take a rejection personally because there are many reasons an agency will not want to represent you that have nothing to do with you or your talent. A very common reason is the company already represents a person with a similar voice and you would be in conflict with present talent. Another reason could be that your strong suit, which may be animation, is not theirs.

You should never take a rejection personally because there are many reasons an agency will not want to represent you that have nothing to do with you or your talent.

Unfortunately, there is also a chance that no one even took the time to listen to your demo. If you feel this has happened to you, I suggest resubmitting the following month. Sometimes the staff who reviewed your demo or dumped it in the trash without a listen the first time you submitted is no longer there. The turnover rate in the agency business is high because of promotions and offers from other agencies. The next group of ears could love your demo and want to sign you.

The size of the agency and its level of power in the industry are important, but you should lean toward a company that seems to be really excited about representing you. You can get lost in the shuffle of a large, powerful agency. A mid-level or boutique (small) agency might give you more attention and be more beneficial to your career.

The entertainment business dictates the laws of the land, and the business says actors must have an agent. Agents have already established relationships with the people you need to meet. Producers and casting directors contact agents when they are looking for voice-over talent, not the talent. You want an agent to afford you the opportunity to audition for any and everything you are right for, and when you book those jobs, you want your agent to make sure that you get paid. The agent normally gets a ten percent commission. Your money comes to the agent first then she sends it to you less her commission fee.

Your contract with an agent can be anywhere from one to three years. I would suggest you only sign for one year initially. In order for agents to make money, they have to get you work. If your agent has met this criterion I'm sure that you will want to sign up again when your contract expires. If you want to terminate your contract early, your agent would have to agree to release you, or if you have not worked in three months, legally the agent has to accept your request to terminate.

Remember, before you sign with any agent or manager, make sure she is franchised (licensed). You can call the union to find out if she is legitimate. Good luck!

THE AGENCY HOUSE REEL

Once you've joined an agency you'll be required to supply a commercial minute for the agency's commercial house reel. This is an agency voice-over demo that has a minute of commercial voice samples from all of the company's talent on one or two CDs. The agency will also include your minute on their website for prospective employers to listen to.

The same engineer who helped you put together the very demo that got you signed can put your commercial minute together for you. If you'd like, you can take a sample of your minute to your agent to make sure you are headed in the right direction in terms of your content, order, and overall pace. Take the suggestions from your agent back to your engineer and finish the demo minute.

It's always a good idea to include your agent in the decision on content and presentation for your demos. It makes her feel involved in your career, and it gives you a chance to get personal attention from your very busy agent.

You may also appear on more than one house reel within the agency if you qualify. For instance if the agency has a promo house reel and you have promo material, you could be eligible for that reel. The animation house reel is another possibility if your agency deems you worthy. The house reel is distributed throughout the industry and can result in bookings, so be sure to submit your best work.

THE AUDITION

There is nothing more attractive in a person than confidence. Some of the most physically unattractive people can persuade you to find them beautiful by exhibiting their complete self-confidence.

When you walk into a room to audition, confidently stride in. Sign in, pick up your copy, and study it. If you believe without a doubt that whatever you're reading for is yours to have, you'll have a better chance of convincing the casting director and the client when they review your taped audition that your voice is the only one to promote the product. Realistically, you can't get every job for which you audition, but a positive and winning attitude will certainly increase your odds for success. When you project a positive attitude, you destroy the competition. Suddenly they can't concentrate on their copy because they are so taken with you. They start to believe you should have the job, and their actions and subsequent inadequate auditions reflect that.

Beware of the actor who has already finished auditioning and wants to engage you in a conversation about the weather or some other trivial matter in an attempt to distract you. Her goal is to interfere with your study process. Don't be fooled. Study your copy. Any actor who would try to sabotage your audition is insecure and most likely threatened by your confidence. You should always be focused on getting the job. The longer you study the copy, the better you're going to be. The old adage "practice makes perfect" most definitely applies to the audition process.

Reading and understanding the direction and character description on your copy is very important. Unless you're told to be subtle and underplay a character, I recommend being energetic or over the top. Give the casting director something to cut back rather than leaving her wanting something more. Some coaches or teachers will tell you that less is more. That may be true for onscreen acting where the camera picks up every facial nuance; however, I find that aggressiveness is the most winning approach in voice-over. Understand what you're reading, and always think real person unless directed otherwise.

While studying the copy, try to isolate yourself from the other actors for maximum concentration.

Try to avoid hearing your competition audition. Sometimes the tryout rooms aren't soundproof and you can hear the other artists auditioning. Don't listen! Other people's auditions could affect you negatively. You don't want to be influenced by someone else's interpretation of the copy.

Before you audition, if you have any questions about the script, don't be afraid to speak up. Most casting directors are more than happy to answer any questions you may have about the script and will encourage you to ask. They want to assess your ability to take direction so make sure you're extra attentive and alert when given direction.

There are some common direction requests that may be asked of you during your audition. Be prepared to respond to:

- ○ **"Do it again, but different."**—You should read the copy over again, changing your rhythm, inflections, and volume this time around.

- ○ **"Give me a little more smile."**—Brighten up your delivery on the next pass. Make it friendlier.

- ○ **"Can you make it less announcery?"**—This means you are too stiff and you're sounding like a newscaster. Read it again like a regular everyday person.

- ○ **"Make it yours."**—Add your own personality to your performance. The director at this point is giving you the chance to be creative and direct yourself. Imagine that you wrote the copy when you read it. Make it sound familiar to you. Own it.

- ○ **"Pick it up."**—Give it more enthusiasm and energy. Be aggressive.

- ○ **"Stay in character."**—If you get this comment it means you have wandered away from the characteristics of the role you are playing. For example, if the character had a stutter and you stopped stuttering, you would be out of character.

When you're done with your audition, ask the casting director if there is any other way she would like you to read the copy. If you have another read in mind, ask if you can read the material again. If your request is denied, don't belabor the point. Say thank you for the opportunity to audition and leave. Be sure to sign out when you leave, especially if you've been at an audition for a long time. AFTRA, the main union and guild covering voice-over artists, will make the casting agency pay you a fee if you're kept waiting at an audition over a certain amount of time. Signing out and listing the time you left will make you eligible.

Although I have never done this, some actors will take the audition copy with them to study and memorize it just in case they get the job. They feel they'll be more prepared when they get to the session. My experience has been that the audition copy seldom turns out to be used in the final session. If you get stuck on the old, you may have trouble adapting to the new, which might be similar or different enough to really confuse you.

Sometimes the producers will put a couple of actors "on avail." This means your agent has to let the producers know you're available for work on the proposed dates of the session. Avail has no legal or contractual status. On the other hand, if the producer books you for a job on a certain date, she has twenty-four hours before that date to release you if she decides not to use you. If she fails to inform you of your release within twenty-four hours, she has to pay you a union scale rate for one commercial spot.

When you're represented by a voice-over agency in California or New York, seventy-five percent of your auditioning will take place there. At really busy times you could audition three to four days a week at the agency. Someone from the agency will call you and give you a time to come in. You will receive your copy when you get there. As you study your copy in the designated actors' area, you wait patiently for your turn in one of the two to three booths to record your audition copy. If you have the equipment at home, you can have your agent fax your copy to you and send your auditions to your agent via the Internet.

The agency puts all of the auditions on one CD and messengers or e-mails them to the client. The client reviews every submission from all of the agencies in the city and makes casting decisions.

Even though you audition more at your agency, you'll book more jobs from your auditions outside. The reason being, when a casting director calls you in for an audition, you're one of a very elite list of actors. The casting director only calls a few actors for a particular part. When you audition at the agency, you're in competition with everyone there, plus all of the other agencies in town. Your odds are not as good.

The audition is very important! Never underestimate its importance. There have been two occasions in my career when the audition turned out to be the "final spot." When I auditioned for my Alpo television spot I never had to do a formal session. They put my taped audition right into the spot. It turned out to be one of my biggest moneymakers. Your audition is your time to shine, so make the most of it.

WHAT CASTING DIRECTORS EXPECT FROM YOU, THE ACTOR

As a successful professional voice-over artist with many years of experience, I have the expertise to advise you about the voice-over business from an actor's perspective. I started this chapter talking to you about the audition process, and I gave you my own views on how you should conduct yourself and what to look out for in an audition. I also talked briefly about what I thought casting directors wanted from you.

Now you will hear from four of the top voice-over casting directors in the Los Angeles area, who were kind enough to contribute their expertise. I asked each one of them to respond to this question: What do you expect from actors when they come in to audition for you? In alphabetical order, here's what they had to say:

Carroll Day Kimble, Carroll Voice Casting

Casting is the art of finding the right actor for a particular role. Basically, that is the job of a casting director. And in order to cast, you must hold auditions. So auditioning becomes a very large part of an actor's job. On an average day, an actor might run around to three or more separate auditions. That means performing for several different casting directors. It doesn't matter how often you audition for a particular casting director or how well you know him or her. . . there are a few things to learn, understand, and remember:

- ○ Never arrive late to an audition unless there is a serious scheduling problem or legitimate emergency. Arriving too early is not a great idea either.

- ○ Know your material. Read it, study it, and prepare as needed for your audition. If you're prepared, you'll know what questions to ask once it's your turn.

- ○ Don't second-guess yourself. You've been called in by the casting director because he or she believes you're what the client is looking for. That's why you're there in the first place.

- ○ It's the casting director's job to supply his client with a variety of great talent. Don't worry about who else might be reading for the same role. Use your time in the lobby to focus on giving it your best.

- ○ Most casting directors enjoy and appreciate actors or they wouldn't be casting in the first place. There should be mutual respect between the actor and the casting director. They need each other to get the job done!

Elaine Craig, Elaine Craig Voice Casting

Prepare for your audition. Primarily what I expect in an audition is for you to be as prepared as possible *before* stepping into the recording booth. To be prepared you need to arrive at the audition at least ten minutes early.

The script or scripts will be posted in the waiting room in most casting offices. After you've read it over to yourself, don't be afraid to ask the office staff questions about direction, pronunciation, etc.

Then you need to find a quiet corner to read it out loud several times. If there is a rough spot that your tongue is tripping over, read that part over and over until you feel completely confident. It is not unlike practicing the piano or any other instrument. Take it one section at a time until you are completely confident with pronouncing all the words, then you can focus on the interpretation.

✓ A quick guide to interpreting the script is: Ask yourself, who are you? where are you? and how do you feel about this product or service? Also, what is your attitude toward other characters in the script if there are others? If the script doesn't have other characters, then focus on imagining who your listener might be. Remember you're always talking to someone. The more specific you are about your choices, the more believable the performance.

If this sounds like basic commercial voice-over 101, that's because it is; however, I'm always amazed at how many people don't take the time to prepare. If you really want to annoy a casting director, simply utter these words upon entering the recording booth: "Oh, I haven't even looked at this yet, let me just take a quick look!" (Okay, I admit, there are times when the casting director might rush you in before you're ready because we're on a time crunch.) But, there are usually two other reasons you aren't prepared. Either you didn't arrive early or you've been socializing in the waiting room instead of reading the script. It's usually the latter.

Actors in the voice-over world are generally a very friendly, very gregarious, fun group of people. That's one of the wonderful things about making a living in this business, it's fun; however, it's also very important to remember that it's a business, both yours and mine, so don't forget why you're there. I know one very successful veteran voice talent who *always* goes outside the waiting room so he can focus and rehearse away from everyone else. He's been doing this his whole career. And guess what? His auditions are always brilliant and he's invited back time after time.

Once you're in the booth, don't be afraid to ask the casting director if there is any special direction. I usually give very little direction before the audition because I want to hear where your instincts take you. I want your audition to be unique to you and not sound like everyone else who walks in the door. Then I may guide you in another direction for a second take, so it's important that you stay flexible. Remember: A casting director is on your side—we want you to shine. If you look good, we look good. And, we know you're talented or you wouldn't have landed in our office in the first place. So always go into your audition prepared and confident and you can't lose. Even if you don't book this one, most likely you will be invited back for another opportunity.

Cathy and "Da Harv" Kalmenson,
Kalmenson & Kalmenson Voice Casting

Every "ballpark" has its own characteristics. We take great pains in order to benefit the actor's performance. The better the actor's performance, the stronger our overall audition will be. Therefore, assume that every piece of printed material set out for the actor has a reason for being there. We don't write instructions or give direction for the purpose of self-aggrandizement, but rather as an aid to secure excellence.

Prior to the Audition:

You Are Responsible

○ Know what product/project you are auditioning for.

○ If the job will be TV, then check for any product conflict *before* confirming you'll be at the audition.

○ Know which role you are auditioning for before you arrive. (Ask your agent or whoever is calling to schedule you.)

○ If you have any issues with endorsing certain products, make sure they are taken into consideration *before* the audition date. (Do not "decline" on the spot at our casting studio. This causes problems for us.)

○ Be aware of work date (record date) and be available. (If you have any conflicts with the work date, communicate them via your agent before confirming your audition, otherwise your audition could be a waste of time for everyone.

During the Audition

○ "On time" means *early*.

○ We run right on time—the tightest ship in town, we're told.

○ Instant accessibility via cell, beeper, agent, etc., is critical.

○ Latecomers may be turned away if they don't communicate their problem in advance. Habitual latecomers will not be called in again.

Voice-over Is an Acting Craft

○ Studying the copy is not only important but *required* in order to give the performance that has a chance to win the job.

○ Ask questions for clarity during your pre-audition study time (pronunciations, etc.).

Prepare

○ Do not ask us "what are they looking for?" Examine the variables presented and then ask yourself "what is it I see?" You are at Kalmenson because we feel your natural characteristics match the casting specs. We're looking for your "truth" in attitude. Nothing put-on unless it's called for.

Have Respect for the Director and Direction

○ When the actor enters the booth, a mic is set, and he or she is focused on the director immediately for an instruction before giving a level. Because direction, storyboards, and any audio/video references were provided in the lobby, both director and actor will focus on the actor's prepared performance followed by director's notes and redirect.

○ Truth rules. Almost anything that supports it is allowed.

○ Ad-libs and improv are welcome, within reason. Human reactions such as sighs, laughs, natural phrases, buttons at the end, etc., are all possibilities, unless we are advised otherwise, then we let the actor know. An additional take is justified only by a change of attitude.

After the Audition

There's no time for playbacks, so don't expect to hear your performance. Upon completion of the booth audition, we prefer the actor leave the premises, maximizing our efficiency so we can maintain excellence throughout our day for our encounters with every actor and so we make our deadlines.

Huck Liggett and Martha Mayakis, The Voicecaster
The most important advice to any aspiring voice-over

talent is to be prepared. Not just for the audition itself, but for the overall process. That means getting the proper training to learn not only the basics of VO, but how to create and develop choices that are best suited to the individual. Each talent has his own strengths, and it is up to him to practice and fine-tune those choices so that when opportunity does present itself, he is ready to deliver without hesitation. Confidence and versatility are always a plus.

One of the biggest misconceptions is that actors feel ready to do voice-overs without ever having had any specific training. As with any other acting medium, there are particular requirements necessary to be competitive. It's not the same approach used for stage and television acting. Choices tend to be a lot subtler. Learning and honing these techniques are essential to voice-over success. Don't just leave it to chance. Get into a reputable voice-over workshop to prepare properly.

Overall, we deal with the most competitive talent in L.A., and to that end our expectations are high. Our clients hire us to select the top voice-over actors for any given project. The people invited to audition at The Voicecaster know they need to come prepared. Specific things we look for at the auditions are:

1. Punctuality—Show up on time. We respect the actors and know their time is valuable to them, we expect the same courtesy in return. Treat this just like any other professional job interview. We attempt to run on time for us as well as you.

2. Professionalism—Confirm your audition time in a timely manner. Call as soon as possible if you are running late or unable to make your appointment. Audition spaces are limited by the client's requirements. If you can't make your appointed time, allow us the opportunity to fill it with another actor. That's a courtesy you would appreciate as well. Not showing up at all puts us in the awkward position of having to explain to our client why we didn't deliver the number of submissions promised.

3. Preparedness—Pay attention to the direction supplied and take the time to read and work through the script before you enter the booth to audition. Don't just wing it. Make specific choices based on all the information supplied (i.e., direction, storyboards, vocal references, timing, and logic of the script). Also be ready to take verbal direction when offered. Learn to listen. Our job is to help you be at your competitive best.

4. Current trends—Be aware of advertising trends and adapt accordingly. Presently one of the most popular requests in ads is for voice-over talents who sound like real people. Simple as that may seem, it is one of the most difficult adjustments for actors to make. There is a great temptation to want to perform. It is refreshing to find talent who knows how to just be themselves.

5. Demos—For most people a demo is the first introduction to the voice-over world. First impressions are very important. Take the time to prepare for what choices you should have on your demo, as well as finding a professional demo producer with the experience and reputation worthy of showing you in your best light. Do not waste your time, money, and effort by attempting to make a demo before you've trained and developed the variation of choices required to show a range of attitudes.

6. New talent—The buzz on the street is that there is too much competition in voice-over and that there's no room for new talent. That couldn't be farther from the truth. We work with clients daily who are eager to hear new voices. The addendum is that these actors need to be at a competitive level. There's the challenge.

Voice-over is a field that allows for a more relaxed and casual atmosphere. However, do not mistake casual for ill preparedness and/or lack of professionalism.

My First Voice-Over Agency

In the summer of 1992, I made a decision that would change the course of my life forever. I decided to expand my horizons. No longer would I pursue my dream to be an actor and singer exclusively. Yes, I still wanted to achieve those lofty goals, but something else kept coming up in my life. That something else was voice-overs.

At first, I didn't even know what voice-overs were. People would constantly say to me, "You have a great voice, you should be doing voice-overs," so I researched the field, took a voice-over class, and set out to make my first demo.

Armed with a two-minute cassette of several well-produced commercial spots that featured my vocal versatility and ability, I proceeded to try and find representation. I submitted my demo to twelve or so agencies in town. Every agency with the exception of one wanted to sign me. I was shocked and very happy. My decision about with whom to sign was made easy since one of the biggest voice-over agencies in Los Angeles wanted to represent me, so I signed with them.

I booked the first audition for which I read and found myself on an airplane to Oakland, California, to record two radio spots for Bank of America. I went on to do tons of commercials for radio and television. I did promos for all the major networks. I landed the role of Joe Robbie Robertson in the animated series *Spider-Man* and I guest starred on many other hit cartoon shows.

CHAPTER 3

The Session

My number one bit of advice for your first voice-over session? Get there early—thirty to forty-five minutes early if possible. The session is no time to be "fashionably late." You might ruffle a few feathers of those who don't like early birds, but I'd rather be "unfashionably early" than late any day. And of course, being on time never got anybody in trouble. I just think the more time you have to work on your script and get acclimated to your surroundings, the better.

In this chapter, you will see sample commercial, promo, trailer, animation, and tag copy. We start with the segment Interpreting Your Copy so that you can better understand how to read the script. I have written all of the material, and the products are fictitious. I have personally participated in thousands of sessions in my voice-over career, so if by chance any of my scripts contain familiar copy or the names of actual products, companies, or characters, my use of them was unintentional, coincidental, and merely a result of my retention of past work. For more sample copy, see Appendix A.

INTERPRETING YOUR COPY

As I have stated before, I got into this business in large part because a number of people kept telling me I had a great sounding voice. That was my impetus, the sound of my voice. I approached each and every job with the goal of sounding good. But as I became more experienced, I realized that success in this business has very little to do with the sound of your voice, it's the way you interpret the copy. Your ability to make the words your own and bring the writer's copy to life is what separates you from the rest of the pack. It is your acting ability that makes you more desirable than the next voice talent. You must approach each piece of copy with the thought *that voice-over is voice acting*.

Many voice-over actors in the business today resent the recent influx of movie stars who are now using their celebrity to win commercial campaigns and character roles in animated features. Yes, their celebrity is probably the reason they were hired, but it's their acting ability that makes them great and makes advertisers continue to covet their services. Tom Hanks as the voice of Woody in *Toy Story* and Eddie Murphy's animation success as the voice of the donkey in *Shrek* is not a surprise—they're great actors. James Earl Jones is a great actor so his voice-over success saying those simple words "This is CNN" is not unexpected. It's not the sound of your voice; it's how you interpret the copy!

If you took a group of ten people and asked each of them to read the same paragraph in a story, then tell you what the paragraph was about, you would get ten slightly different descriptions. Even though it seems obvious to everyone what the author was trying to convey in this paragraph, given the various interpretations, it is not so obvious after all.

There will probably also be at least one interpretation that is so much more colorful and exciting than the paragraph itself, you'll wonder if that person read the same thing everyone else did. Some voice-over artists are just better than others when it comes to interpreting commercial copy. Their ability to take their interpretation of the script and create a delivery that is both more entertaining and imaginative than their competitions' is the reason they book the jobs.

When you receive your audition copy or your copy on the job, the first thing you should do is read the voice-over direction and the character description at the top of the page. Understanding and interpreting the voice-over direction will help you interpret the copy. Every word in the direction is important. Here's a sample of some announcer direction for a thirty-second TV promo for a video game.

TRON TV :30 VO Direction: *Voice should be male, deep, and gravelly with a dark and ominous quality. Read Darth Vader. Or maybe slightly nuts á la Jerry Lewis.*

Okay, now let's interpret the VO direction. First, take into account the time of the spot, thirty seconds (:30). What this tells us is that whatever the copy consists of, the spot as a whole is only thirty seconds. Now you have an overall time parameter.

Next we will give equal importance to the literal meaning of each descriptive word. *Voice should be male* is self-explanatory. *Deep* means speak in your lower register. *Gravelly* would be considered a low-pitched vocal direction, weighty, somber maybe. *With a dark and ominous quality* means the announcer should sound threatening or menacing. *Read Darth Vader* confirms our interpretation of what your read should sound like—dark and evil. *Or maybe slightly nuts á la Jerry Lewis* is an indication the producers are simply giving you an option to go another way.

Now let's dissect the actual copy.

TRON TV :30

Is there a Heaven?

Is there a Hell.

There is one powerful force who knows the answers . . . all too well.

When you're caught between Heaven and Hell, make 'em both suffer.

Tron: Doomsday, rated "M" for Mature.

The first line *Is there a Heaven?* feels majestic. Keeping in mind the VO direction, you must sound majestic in a dark and ominous way.

The second line *Is there a Hell.* may perplex you because you think a question mark should be at the end of this sentence but there's a period. Is this a typo? Let's assume you can't get a definitive answer, so you make the choice to read it like a question. Now you're being imaginative.

Remember, your goal is to find the interpretation that will motivate the listener to buy the product you are selling with your voice.

There is one powerful force who knows the answers . . . all too well. Your first thought should be who knows the answers all too well? You surmise that the hero Tron is the powerful one who knows it all, so your vocal intensity increases on this line because you're halfway to the money line—the title.

The fourth line *When you're caught between Heaven and Hell, make 'em both suffer* is what this whole thing is all about—it's the plot, the conflict, and your chance to be like Darth Vader, dark and evil. We should be able to feel the pain when your gravelly voice resonates on the word *suffer*. Now you're being entertaining.

The copywriter has restricted your creativity with the line, *Tron: Doomsday, rated "M" for Mature*, which is obviously a takeoff on the movie trailers we all know and love where the voice-over ends the trailer with "Rated R for mature audiences. Children under seventeen not admitted without parent." It probably wouldn't be too smart to deviate from the obvious trailer delivery here. Of course you could go nuts á la Jerry Lewis.

The more you practice the techniques of breaking down copy, the quicker those techniques become habit.

In Review

You always want to study and understand the VO direction and character description before you try to interpret the copy. When you get to the copy, use the three *w*'s to assist you in your understanding of the character. Who is my character? What is my character's motivation? Where does my character fit in this story?

When you want to find the best read to sell a commercial product. Here are some choices to consider:

○ **The Flat Read**—You should read the copy with as little expression and energy as possible. Give each word equal importance, and your rhythm should be very even.

○ **The Sarcastic Read**—You should have a wry, cocky, and slightly rude personality in your delivery. Say every word with a raised eyebrow and a wink. The copy must call for this approach.

○ **High-Energy Read**—With a burst of energy, you dive into the copy and deliver it with excitement.

○ **Hard Sell**—This is a loud, in-your-face, boisterous read. It can also be soft, but it's always in-your-face and intense.

○ **Soft Sell**—A quieter and more intimate read. You don't have to push.

○ **Real Person Read**—Throw out all of your voice-over technique and just read the copy. Be natural. Talk the way you talk in everyday life. This is the read most advertisers are looking for today, and the toughest for most voice-over actors to pull off. Just make it conversational.

Go to Appendix A and practice some of the sample commercial copy, using the different types of sell approaches.

COMMERCIAL SESSIONS

Hopefully copy will be available immediately or shortly after your arrival to the studio. Take these precious moments to study the script. Before the session starts, make sure you write down the names of your engineer and the director somewhere on your copy—I usually write them in the upper right hand corner of the first page. These are the two people with whom you will talk during the session when you are behind the glass clad in your headphones, so you want to know their names.

Once the engineer has set you up at the microphone, start mentally rehearsing the script. If you are working with other actors, as a group you all may choose to rehearse the script aloud. If that is the case, be a trouper and rehearse with the group.

If I am alone, I don't want the director to hear me read the copy before I record unless he asks to hear me. My rehearsal reads should not be judged negatively or positively because I'm in practice mode. What I do while warming up is not necessarily what I'm going to do when I record. So, in my opinion, the director should not hear your voice until the engineer asks you for a level (an indication of how loud you will speak in the microphone). And don't give away too much on that level check either; reserve the "real deal" for the first take (the first time you record) and all of those that follow. After the first take the director can assess where you are going and direct you accordingly.

Occasionally the studio may be pretty crowded when you enter. Be prepared to possibly have to be introduced to the writer of the commercial, the director, engineer, and several other representatives from the advertising agency, so as always, be on your best behavior.

While the session is in progress don't be surprised if you find yourself being directed by several people in the room, all giving you different suggestions about how to interpret your copy. Stay patient and positive, and remember, the clients are always right. They are paying you top dollar to read the copy the way they want it read. Believe me, there are worse things you could be doing. Standing in front of a microphone and creating commercial magic that will potentially pay you thousands of dollars in residuals is a blessing. Your face should always be stuck in smile mode.

When the director is happy and ends the session, let that be the end. I used to have the bad habit of asking if I could do, "one more for me." There were a couple of things wrong with my request. First, it's not about something for me, it is always about what the director or the client wants. Second, if I do something new they really love, the session starts all over again with as many takes as I did the first way. It opens up a whole can of new worms.

Even at the end of a session when the director says, "We're very happy with what we have, is there any other way that you might do it differently?" Say no. I learned the hard way. If they like it, it's good. Leave!

There will be some commercial sessions that will be phone patches. In these types of situations the director is at another location directing you over the phone through your headset. The only people in the studio are the talent and the engineer.

Bring your own room-temperature bottled water to the session to prevent dry mouth. Ice-cold water is too harsh on the vocal cords. Most studios will supply you with water, but you can't depend on it so be prepared.

Take a look at this single-voice commercial copy written to be read by one person. Follow the VO direction and read it out loud a few times until you feel comfortable and satisfied with your read.

:60 TV COMMERCIAL COPY

VO Direction: Straight spirited promo read.

ON JANUARY 15th

GET READY FOR THE NEXT CHAPTER IN HIS COMPELLING STORY

THE LEGEND OF RENNY E. FRANKLIN

THE NEW ALBUM FROM THE INCREDIBLE, EIGHT-TIME GRAMMY-WINNING ARTIST

THE LEGEND OF RENNY E. FRANKLIN FEATURES THE CHART-TOPPING SMASH

"BABY, IT'S HARD TO STOP"

(FADE UP MUSIC)

PLUS "TAKE THE TIME TO LOVE HER"

AND THE PHENOMENAL "I CAN'T BE ALONE TONIGHT"

FOR A LIMITED TIME, THE CD FEATURES A FREE BONUS DVD WITH RENNY AS YOU'VE NEVER SEEN HIM BEFORE!

THE LEGEND OF RENNY E. FRANKLIN IN STORES JANUARY 15th

ON CREAM RECORDS/BBT CDs, CASSETTES AND A SPECIAL LIMITED-EDITION LP

THE LEGEND OF RENNY E. FRANKLIN, JANUARY 15th

(FADE UP MUSIC)

This multiple voice copy is designed to be read by an ensemble.

:60 RADIO COMMERCIAL COPY

VO: Direction. The announcer should be friendly and warm. The people are everyday people on the street.

(MELLOW JAZZ MUSIC UNDER THROUGHOUT)

ANNCR: When you walk into a bank, you expect quality service.

1st MAN: The tellers in this bank are so polite.

ANNCR: At North Star Bank we respect your precious time.

1st WOMAN: I never wait in long lines when I come here.

ANNCR: North Star Bank offers incredibly low-rate loans.

2nd MAN: That's music to my ears!

ANNCR: Plus, with a large deposit you get free checking and free online banking.

1st MAN: I'm up to my ears in debt.

ANNCR: Our financial advisors will help you consolidate your bills.

2nd WOMAN: I would love to open my own hair salon someday.

ANNCR: Let us help you make your small business dreams come true.

2nd MAN: This is a great bank!

ANNCR: We aim to please.

1st WOMAN: I'm very satisfied.

ANNCR: North Star Bank. Come see us today.

Legal Tag: Minimum opening deposit required. Subject to credit approval. One free personal checking account per household. Customary monthly maintenance fees may apply. Equal housing lender. Member FDIC.

TRAILER SESSIONS

A trailer is a vocal narration underneath film clips promoting an upcoming film. If you are one of the rare few to be in a trailer session, you have already far exceeded your fellow voice-over brethren. The same rules used in commercial sessions apply, generally speaking. But when you have achieved trailer status you are truly one among an elite group. The way you sound and act are unique to you. Those individual attributes are the reason you're there in the first place.

There are not a lot of cooks in the kitchen at a trailer session. Normally, it's just you, the director, and the engineer. The cooks are the motion picture studio bosses who listen to your reads later and decide what spots will go to final (be seen by the public). Once that decision is made, the public will get to see those trailers in theaters and on televisions across the country. I love every aspect of doing voice-over work, but if someone said to me, "Rodney, you can only do one kind of voice-over for the rest of your career," I'd choose trailers hands down.

Monetary compensation for guys who do trailers is whatever the market will bear, and believe me when I tell you, the market bears a lot. Generally there are no residuals for trailers; the upfront money reflects the fact that nothing's coming later so "give me a lot now." Trailer voice-over performers are some of the highest paid talent in the industry. Your approach to a piece of trailer copy is based upon the movie genre. The light comedy dictates a happy-smile type of read. The dramatic, dark movie requires a more intense-serious type of read. To help create the comedy read, you can simply smile while reading your copy. To achieve the more dramatic read, deliver your lines with a sense of quiet intimacy. Your rhythm should be even with very little difference in inflection on each word, almost monotone. Remember, you don't have to shout to be dramatic or intense. Get closer to the microphone and let your voice do all of the work. You can practice the dramatic trailer read with this sample trailer copy below.

MIND RAIDERS TRAILER COPY

VO Direction: Dramatic trailer read. Intense.

A MAD SCIENTIST

OUT TO PROVE HIS WORTH TO THE WORLD

AN AVERAGE ATHLETE

WHO WANTS TO BE A SUPERSTAR

TOGETHER THEY WILL SEARCH FOR VICTIMS

AND TAKE THEIR MINDS

THIS HOLIDAY SEASON
HIDE YOUR THOUGHTS
HIDE YOUR FEARS
HIDE YOUR MIND

FROM THE DIRECTOR OF *WILD GEESE DON'T FLY*
JAMES GUNERY
DREW DOMDONAVICH
AND INTRODUCING CLAY REED

MIND RAIDERS

DIRECTED BY ANTONIO FARRELLI
RATED PG-13
AMERICA ONLINE KEYWORD MIND RAIDERS

PROMO SESSIONS

A promo is a recorded announcement promoting a production on television and radio. These sessions can be like commercial sessions when they take place at one of the usual recording studios around town. But when you go to one of the big networks like ABC, NBC, CBS, or FOX, the process is totally different from any recording experience. If you are the "voice of" a network, you enjoy a certain calm that comes with knowing you will read hundreds of promos a month and thousands a year for that network. On the other hand, if you are rarely there, essentially, you are auditioning for your full-time network gig, every time you get your turn at the microphone.

When you drive up to the guard gate at one of the networks, your first thought may be, *Will the guard have a pass for me to get on the lot?* After that you may hope the guards have the correct spelling of your name. Through the years, you may be at this studio lot a whole bunch, but you still are not the "voice of," so occasionally, your name may not be spelled right.

Once you are on the lot, you may feel like a kid at Disneyland for the first time. Your adrenaline is pumping; you can't wait to get into that hot seat in front of the microphone. Nine times out of ten you were hired to do what producers think you do best, so the session will be a breeze based on your expertise in reading these types of promos. When the heads of the on-air promo department at the network agreed on the final promo scripts for the show you are about to promote, your name formed on their lips before the ink dried on the printed copies. "Get Rodney Saulsberry, he did this type of show for us the last time," one of them might say. What is "old hat" for them is an opportunity of a lifetime for you.

After you are handed the copy, the producer of the spots will ask you to take a look at them on a monitor. After your look, take the copy into the announcer's booth. I like to stand when I do voice-overs but it's not cool to stand in this studio. Everything is set up for you to sit down—you couldn't stand if you wanted to. You give the engineer a level (a sample of your vocal volume) and you're off to the races. It's Shakespeare to you and just another promo to them, so speed is of the essence.

There are other announcers scheduled shortly after you, which means hurry up. Don't get me wrong, perfection is the goal, and that sentiment is the intent of everyone involved, but you have to achieve that goal—quickly. Once you're done, sign your contract, say your good-byes, and leave.

Were you so great that the heads of on-air promo want to sign you and make you the new voice of the network? That remains to be seen.

Here's a sample of some promo copy. Follow the voice-over direction and practice, practice, practice.

TV PROMO COPY

VO Direction: Fast-paced promo announcer read.

IT'S A STAR-STUDDED TRIBUTE TO YOUR FAVORITE ARTISTS

BONNIE NOWLES

TYREEK

QUEEN MABALEE

MARY J. BARNES

DAVE CHAPPERELL

MOS DEEP

VERONICA A. FAUX

TAYE DICKERSON

SPECIAL MUSICAL PERFORMANCES AND MORE!

Sot: this is fly!

TREVOR BENSON HOSTS

THE 2003 MASON AWARDS

ANIMATION SESSIONS

The best way to describe an animation session would be to call it simply animated. When you assemble a cast of actors to voice cartoon characters, you end up with quite an energetic session. Your joyful time kibitzing in the lobby with fellow cast members will be followed by even more joy in the session. Be prepared to have a lot of fun.

Shortly after you have been cast, a script will be sent to your home. This gives you the opportunity to familiarize yourself with your lines and to read the script a few times to get a better understanding of how your character fits into the storyline.

Many voice-over artists upon receiving the script will immediately look for all the scenes their character is in and only read and study those scenes. That is a mistake. Inevitably, you will miss a line in the session, causing possible embarrassment. Actors pride themselves on the "cold read" (reading the copy perfect the first time you see it) but when you're in a studio with an ensemble of seasoned, well-trained animation voice artists, you don't want to screw up because you didn't do something as simple as read your entire script before you came to the session.

The union contract also allows for producers to cast you in roles outside of your main character. If you have been assigned additional roles, this increases the importance of reading the entire script and being familiar with everything your characters do.

When you go into the studio, your name will be written on a card that is placed on the music stand alongside your "new" final script. The engineer will come in the room and ask you if you want to stand or sit during the session and adjust your microphone accordingly. I always choose to stand in a session. No matter what genre I'm working in, I just feel that my diaphragm (the muscular partition between the chest and abdominal cavities) supports my voice best when I'm standing. In my opinion, sitting constricts the muscles that support your voice. Being a professional singer and actor, that's what I was always taught; however, I must admit that some very famous voice-over artists prefer sitting, and they have been very successful doing so.

Back behind the mixing board the engineer will go down the line for a vocal level from each artist. Many artists will read one or two of their lines from the script in the voice of the character. Others will choose to say whatever clever thing comes to mind to evoke laughter. When the sound check is completed the director slates (speaks the date, name of the show, episode number, and take number) the session into a microphone from the control room and the session begins.

I have been on shows where you do the complete show once, break, and come back for pickups (redoing some of your lines) if needed. On one level it may be great to hear you were perfect and no pickups for any of your lines were necessary. On the other hand, you may hate to be released because you were having so much fun.

When it comes to animation, the question I am asked most often by the public is how do you get your voice to fit so perfectly into the mouths of the animation figures? Or, are you looking at the cartoon characters on a screen while you work? The answer is the animators (artists who draw the cartoon characters) match the animation to the actors' dialogue. In other words, on most occasions, the voices come first. In fact, there have been a few occasions when my own mouth and facial expressions have been videotaped and used to influence the look of the character to whom I am giving voice.

Technique in animation is very important. Just the sounds you have to make to sell falling off a building, taking a punch, or even breathing is a process that must be taught or learned. Your natural talent will take you a long way in some areas of voice-over, but you will increase your chances of booking more animation sessions if you take animation classes.

Here's a sample animation script. You should play a different character each time you read it. If you can find a partner, read it together then read it again, switching roles. Males can play females and vice versa, if you have the ability. The challenge is a good exercise.

ANIMATION SCRIPT COPY

VO Direction: Play all characters over the top, but make them real people, no cartoon voices.

INT. BARBERSHOP

UNCLE TOOKIE the fat barber is cutting his thirteen-year-old nephew WINKIE'S hair. Above the loud R&B

music on the radio, we hear him trying to teach the young fellow about the birds and the bees when he is suddenly interrupted and surprised by the kid's knowledge and experience...

UNCLE TOOKIE
You did what?

WINKIE
I put my tongue . . .

UNCLE TOOKIE
(Cutting him off) Boy, I will take these clippers and cut your tongue out your mouth. You too young to be kissin' girls already. Don't you talk like that in my barbershop!

WINKIE
I'm sorry, Uncle Tookie.

WIDEN TO REVEAL entire room. There are only two barber chairs in this shop located in the basement of UNCLE TOOKIE and his wife, MABLE'S home. A sign above the mirrors behind the chairs reads "Tookie & Mable's Basement Barbershop."

MABLE
What are you hollering about now, Tookie? And why is this music so loud? You can't even hear yourself think.

MABLE stops working on the customer's head she's cutting and walks over to the radio to turn it down. She's even fatter than UNCLE TOOKIE so her buttocks knock over a few items in her path.

WINKIE

Uncle Tookie was trying to teach me the facts of
life, so I told him about the time I kissed
Charmaine—

MABLE

(Raising her clipper-toting hand toward WINKIE)
Winkie! I swear, if you ever talk like that again I
will seriously hurt my sister's only son. Where did
you learn to talk so dirty, boy?

WINKIE

My momma.

UNCLE TOOKIE

(To Mable) Your sister! I ain't surprised.

MABLE

Now don't you start on my sister this morning,
Tookie.

UNCLE TOOKIE

I'd have to get in line if I wanted to get started on
her.

MABLE

Hush your mouth!

UNCLE TOOKIE

She ain't raising this boy right. How can she?
Working in a club and doing them lap dances for
money and—

As we do an EXTREME PULL BACK we see the reason
UNCLE TOOKIE can't continue his verbal assault on
WINKIE'S sexy voluptuous mother SONJA. She enters
the room scantily dressed wearing high-heeled platform
shoes.

SONJA

You 'bout finished with my boy, Tookie? I've got places to go and people to see.

TOOKIE rolling his eyes and muttering to himself.

UNCLE TOOKIE

I bet you do.

SONJA

How you doin', Mable?

MABLE

I'm fine, Sonja. How are you this morning?

SONJA

Girl, I'm doin' great. I met me a fine man last night at the club. He's takin' me and Winkie to lunch today.

UNCLE TOOKIE

(With sarcasm) What were you doin' when you met him, Sonja, sittin' in his lap?

SONJA

Now don't start with me this morning, fat man!

At first, Mable tries to be a calming force.

MABLE

You two need to stop carrying on like this in front of the boy. (Pause) Who you callin' fat? Girl, I will take these clippers and cut your fake—

UNCLE TOOKIE

Hey, hey, not in front of the boy! (To Sonja) I'm finished with Winkie's hair. You can go now, Miss Sonja.

Sonja tries to pay Tookie for the haircut.

                    UNCLE TOOKIE
That's alright, Sonja. Keep it. I don't want to touch
last night's tip money.

                       SONJA
Whatever. C'mon, Winkie. Cecil's taking us to
McDonald's. We can't be late.
                                        FADE OUT.

            END OF SHOW

DEMOS

There will be times when you'll be booked to work on a
commercial that is not meant to be aired. This demonstration is usually created by an advertising agency trying
to acquire an account. If the client likes the demo, the
agency will get the job.

The demo is purely a speculative venture, and is also
known as working on "spec" in the industry. Demos are
not supposed to air, so performers are paid a lower fee. If
the demo is upgraded (becomes a regular commercial)
and airs, the actor is paid more.

SCRATCH TRACKS

The unfinished version of a commercial, promo, or
trailer is called a scratch track. It's the guide track a director asks you to watch or listen to before you add your
voice to a spot in a session. The voice you hear on the
scratch track is usually an engineer, producer, or the

writer of the spot. You should only listen to the voice for the sake of getting the timing correct, but don't emulate this unprofessional performance. You are the professional, and that is why you were hired.

You can find the union pay rates for all of the sessions in the Money section of Chapter Six.

TAGS

A tag is the final line you hear at the end of a commercial, promo, or trailer.

Commercial tag: "Get your big mouth jug at a Target near you."

Promo tag: "Tonight on FOX 5."

Trailer tag: "Under seventeen not admitted without parent."

You can find more tags in Appendix A.

LEGAL TAGS

These fast-paced and quickly read lines give legal information or disclaimers about the product that is barely audible at the end of a commercial spot.

A legal tag: (FAST) "Advertised price is MSRP less
$1,500 limited-time factory rebate. Excludes freight,
taxes, title, license, and options. Dealer price may vary.
Comparison of MSRP of comparably equipped Sonata
Free and Toga RAV5 including freight; excluding taxes,
title, and license. See dealer for limited warranty details."

A tag session can be very lucrative. You get the union
rate for each one, along with the session fee just for
showing up. I have been in trailer sessions where I have
read more than fifteen tags for three hundred and sev-
enty dollars a tag plus the session fee. Your trailer tag rate
is negotiable.

My Trailer Love Affair

There is nothing quite like the rush of sitting in a theater watching the coming attraction trailers and hearing your own voice booming out of the speakers. And oh boy! If I hear myself twice on two different movies back to back, stick me with a fork, this turkey is done!

If you are lucky enough to be "the voice" of an entire campaign for a major multimillion-dollar motion picture, for about two weeks you will hear yourself on television, radio, and the Internet all day and night long.

The first trailer I ever worked on was Spike Lee's *Crooklyn.* I put a lot of effort into convincing Universal Pictures to use my voice to promote one of their movies. I did what I do: I made numerous telephone calls, sent every producer in the trailer department a copy of my demo, made contact with the assistants and secretaries of each producer, and seized the opportunity when it presented itself.

You never forget your first trailer, especially when it's a big one like *Crooklyn.*

After I got the first campaign I thought the second one would be easier to get, but it wasn't. In 1995, my agents and I had to work doubly hard to get Ice Cube's first installment of *Friday* from New Line Cinema.

I really hit my stride in 1998 when I was chosen to promote the romantic drama *How Stella Got Her*

Groove Back from Twentieth Century Fox. One night I had the pleasure of sitting in some great seats at a Lakers basketball game with a friend of mine when the *Stella* trailer popped up on the big screen on center court at halftime. What a surprise. I never dreamed of hearing my voice at a professional basketball game.

Now with a number of movies under my belt, my goals began to change. How cool would it be to promote the number one movie in America? I found out on October 22, 1999, when Universal's *The Best Man* opened at the number one spot. I voiced the entire campaign. I was ecstatic and so was Universal. They showed me their appreciation by using me on another movie that same year, the Eddie Murphy/Steve Martin comedy *Bowfinger*.

It's hard to remember what came next, but once it became apparent to the industry that I was a "player" in the trailer world, my resume got really long, really fast. I also started to get attention from the national print media. In 1999, *Black Enterprise* magazine wrote, "Saulsberry has the voice of choice for behind-the-scene narration." In 2000, *Upscale* magazine declared mine "A voice to be reckoned with," and in 2002, *Savoy* magazine wrote, "Saulsberry is the voice-over man of choice for black cinema."

My other trailer campaigns include *The Players Club, Original Gangstas, Clockers, Life, Soul Food, Hav Plenty, White Man's Burden, Bamboozled, All*

About the Benjamins, Hardball, Juwanna Mann, Friday After Next, Undercover Brother, Finding Forrester, Foolish, Kingdom Come, BAPS, Drumline, Dumb & Dumberer, Dysfunktional Family, Tupac Resurrection, Against the Ropes, and many more.

I've said it before and I'll say it again: I love doing trailers.

CHAPTER 4

Voice-Over Work Outside the Norm

W hen I started in this business the opportunities for employment were limited to television and radio. In a field that was already small in terms of the number of successful actors making a living, only two forms of media to work in was tough. Due to the recent popularity of doing voice-over work, competition is even stronger; however, today there are many more media outlets. We're going to explore some of these areas.

RADIO IMAGING

Many radio stations hire a talent to do all of their IDs, promos, liners, and sweepers. This "voice of the station" represents its image. If you are interested in getting work in this area, you will need a radio imaging demo, which is very different from the others we have covered. It should be no longer than one minute. The content depends on what radio format you are trying to get work in. Once you decide which format or formats you want to pursue, the music and the copy you use should be geared toward that choice. Some of the formats you can choose include: CHR, Contemporary Hit Radio, formerly called the Top Forty; Classic Rock; AC, Adult Contemporary; Urban AC; Oldies; Country; Alternative; Modern Rock; Hot AC; News/Talk; and Jazz.

Finding someone to produce this kind of demo for you is kind of tricky. The same person who produced your commercial demo is probably more than capable of producing a promo, trailer, or animation one. But most of these same directors and producers haven't a clue as to how to construct a radio imaging demo. You have to really do your homework and search for someone who has a lot of experience in this field.

When I decided to chase this form of voice-over, I was told to hire a professional radio deejay to produce my demo. A disc jockey has the proper equipment, copy, sound effects, and the ability to use cross-fade (raising the level of one sound and lowering another simultaneously) techniques with echo and reverb, and the ears to give me the best demo possible. Try to find someone who truly has knowledge of the genre. I listened to that good advice and got a demo with which I am very happy. You can go online and find many production companies that specialize in producing radio image demos, and their costs are fairly reasonable at $150 to $300 per demo.

Your agent may or may not be interested in representing you in this area because it doesn't pay a whole lot of money per job. The ideal situation would be to have a number of accounts across the country that pay you a monthly fee for your services. I know artists who supply as many as twenty stations across the country with IDs, dry voice-over commercials, sweepers, and liners every month via ISDN or an e-mail-delivered MP3. Each station pays them anywhere from three to five hundred dollars a month.

Get yourself a list of program directors who make the hiring and firing decisions at the radio station. First you should solicit the local stations in your immediate area. After you exhaust that market, take your campaign to a national level by sending your demo to radio stations across the United States. Hopefully the program directors will listen to your demo and consider you for work.

There are some avenues to consider outside of your agency. Companies like VoiceHunter.com specialize in getting radio imaging work for their VO talent. This company has a house CD that has more than seventy-five hundred voices on it. Its web presence is heavy, and it's one of the leading free voice casting services in the country. VoiceHunter.com has placed many of its artists on radio stations across the country including ABC, Citidel, and Clear Channel. Contact information can be found in the Resources section of this book. For more information on other companies that specialize in this field, go on the Internet and type in "radio imaging."

To get a feel for this genre, practice reading this sample radio imaging copy below. Have fun with it.

RADIO IMAGING COPY

VO Direction: A fast-paced energetic read. Give it a radio deejay feel.

STARTING TODAY! THE WJAM HOOKIN' YOU UP FOR THE HOLIDAYS CONTEST IS HERE. FOUR DAYS, THREE NIGHTS FOR TWO ADULTS. YOU CHOOSE FROM OVER ONE HUNDRED AND FIFTY DIFFERENT LOCATIONS IN THE U.S. AND CANADA. STAY IN TOP-NOTCH HOTELS LIKE THE HILTON, DOUBLETREE, AND MARRIOTT. YOU GET THERE, WJAM PUTS YOU UP, AND HERE'S THE BEST PART: THERE WILL BE FOUR WINNERS AND QUALIFY-ING IS SIMPLE. JUST BE THE TWENTIETH CALLER TO THE WJAM HOT LINE EVERY DAY FROM NOW THROUGH FRIDAY DECEMBER 5th AND YOU'RE AUTOMATICALLY ENTERED. STAYS MUST BE USED BY DECEMBER 31st. THE WJAM PUTTIN' YOU UP FOR THE HOLIDAYS CONTEST, FROM THE STATION THAT HOOKS YOU UP ON A REGULAR BASIS! WJAM HIP-HOP & R&B!

Voice Prompts

The prerecorded messages that guide a caller through telephone applications are known as voice prompts. If you work in this capacity you would prerecord text like, "Welcome to customer service. All of our agents are busy at this time. Please hold the line. If you are not calling from a touch-tone phone, or if you would like to speak with a customer service representative, please hold and one will be with you shortly." A company could hire you to be their prerecorded auto attendant voice to direct their callers through their phone and voice mail systems. This may be a weekly job if the company changes its voice mail regularly.

One of the most successful companies in the voice prompts field is GM Voices, which specializes in speech recognition technology. Based in Alpharetta, Georgia, this company has been a leader in the field of producing audio programming services for telecommunications and Internet applications for more than ten years. The Great Voice Company in Englewood Cliffs, New Jersey, and Worldly Voices, LLC, are two more employment opportunities for voice talent anywhere in the country with a home studio and ISDN capabilities. For addresses and phone numbers of these three companies, refer to Appendix C.

There are no guarantees, but you should at least check into these employment opportunities. If they don't have work for you immediately, at least your demo submission will be in their database.

You could also be hired to read navigational text. Satellite navigation is the craze these days, and companies specializing in GPS navigation systems need good voice-over talent to make it easy for the consumer to follow the directions while driving.

You can speak for banks, credit card companies, or educational facilities—there are plenty of opportunities. If you speak a foreign language, there are companies who need voice prompts in various languages.

Go online and type in "voice prompt" and a list of companies that specialize in audio programming services for telecommunications will appear. These companies help businesses around the world. They need voice-over talent on their rosters to present to their clients.

You can speak for banks, credit card companies, or educational facilities–there are plenty of opportunities .

Imitate the voice prompts that you've heard before when you practice with the copy below. You must be very clear and professional with a real person quality.

Voice Prompt Copy

VO Direction: A polite professional read.

VO: 1

Welcome to customer service. All of our agents are busy at this time. If you are not calling from a touch-tone phone, or if you would like to speak with a customer service representative, please hold and one will be with you shortly.

VO: 2

If you know the extension of the party you are trying to reach, press one.

For our company directory, press two.

For sales, press three.

For technical support, press four.

To return to the main menu, press five.

LOOPING ADR (AUTOMATED DIALOGUE REPLACEMENT)

When a filmed or taped production is completed and parts of the dialogue soundtracks need to be rerecorded by an actor, that process is called looping. The actor stands in front of a screen and watches her image while listening to dialogue that she has to replace through her headphones. After watching repeatedly, she takes a stab at replacing the words in perfect sync. Some well-known movie stars have been known to mumble or purposely screw their lines up in production so that they can fix it later in a looping session where they can spend more time finessing their dialogue.

Looping is also used to enhance a filmed or taped soundtrack. The actors who gather in a studio to sweeten a movie's soundtrack are called a loop group. There's a lot of money in loop group looping. My first voice-over experience came from my days as a group looper. I worked on a show called In the *Heat of the Night*. The star of the show was the late Carroll O' Connor of *All in the Family* fame. His co-star was the late Howard Rollins. For three years I did all of the dialogue replacement for

Howard. Stars of a weekly drama series rarely come in for incidental words that were shabbily recorded in production. If you are lucky enough to be part of a loop group that has a weekly show, and you are the designated replacement voice for a regular character, you'll make some good money. Each loop group actor signs a contract that pays the SAG minimum per show. A full season run for most prime-time dramas is twenty-two episodes. Plus, you get paid the same amount for the first rerun of each episode.

During my looping years I was fortunate enough to have worked on most of the episodes of such hits as *Tour of Duty*, *China Beach*, and *The Big Easy*. I have also worked on many movies, including, *Money Talks*, *The Hurricane*, *Glory*, *Spider-Man*, *Dr. Doolittle*, *Life*, and *Independence Day*.

Single actors within a loop group will occasionally replace dialogue from a single actor, but the majority of the group's work involves adding crowd ambience to various scenes throughout the production. A group of six or more actors gather in a studio with headphones as they watch the scene they are going to enhance. A number of microphones used for creating an inside or outside effect while recording are placed in strategic areas in front of the actors to pick up their voices. The actors hear a series of three beeps in their headphones. On the imaginary fourth beep the actors began to talk, cheer, scream, or whatever they are instructed to do.

This is yet another form of employment for the voice-over actor. Looping is available almost exclusively in

Hollywood and New York. Do your homework, get contact information on the ADR coordinators of each loop group, and submit your material to them. Sometimes a voice-over demo is required but most often a picture and acting résumé is all that is needed.

NARRATION

If telling a great story is your forté then you might be interested in trying to get narration work. Narration is assimilating information and retelling it. Simply put, it's the art of storytelling. There are many media presentations that require voice-over narration—flash presentations, tutorials, training videos, documentaries, industrials, corporate presentations, trade show videos, CD-ROMs, and the most sought-after form of narrative work by voice-over artists: audiobooks.

Audiobooks are very popular today. Some people would rather listen to a book read by a talented voice actor than read the book themselves. Audiobooks are very convenient because you can listen to them on your way to work, while working out at the gym, or at home. Recently, authors of some of the more popular books have started to read their own audiobooks, in effect taking work away from voice-over professionals. There is also a strong trend lately to get celebrities to read books. Not to worry, there is still plenty of audiobook work available.

To be in contention for any of this narration work, you should have a narration demo. It should consist of:

more than one selection to show your versatility and breadth, a fictional one-page story with characters and accents, a monologue, and some poetry if you excel in those areas.

If you read an audiobook, the fees vary. Your agent can get you anywhere from a few hundred to four thousand dollars. Even the celebrities get a lot less than they are accustomed. They usually get about four to five thousand dollars per book. They take the work for its prestige value.

Be prepared to work three to five hours per session. When I did O. J. Simpson's book, *I Want to Tell You,* for Warner Audio Books, it took us two three-hour sessions to complete it.

My professionalism and training served me well. I had the stamina to sound at the ends of each session just like I sounded at the beginning. This made it easy for the engineer to edit the two sessions together. When I read Sheila Weller's *Raging Heart* for Dove Audio Books, we did the entire book in one six-hour session. That was tough and tiresome work but I thoroughly enjoyed it.

Another form of narration to consider is documentaries. A documentary is a film or television program that presents the facts about a person or event. The voice-over actor you hear is the narrator. I had the pleasure of narrating the Marvin Gaye biography for the E! *True Hollywood Story.* The two-hour television special was an honor for me to narrate because I have always been a big fan of Marvin Gaye's music and the man. It took a couple of hours to finish the session. And although his rise to fame was a joy to tell, it was difficult to narrate his tragic end.

Documentary narration is very popular within the voice-over community. Here is a sample of a documentary style narration. You should work on being very natural and relaxed when you practice this copy. You don't want to sound like an announcer. Act as if you are telling a story to a friend.

NARRATION COPY

VO Direction: A warm storytelling style.

In the early sixties music was changing fast. Gone were the days of rock and roll as we once knew it. Out with the old and in with the new Soul Music. The Motown sound was alive and well in Detroit, the Motor City, but it wasn't the only record company putting out soulful hits and developing black superstars. Stax Records in Memphis, Tennessee, was a force to be reckoned with. Otis Redding, Isaac Hayes, and Sam & Dave are just a few of the many dynamite performers to emerge from the Stax music stable. At one time in the early seventies, Memphis was known as the fourth largest recording center in the world.

WEBSITE VOICE IMAGING

Website voice imaging is fast becoming quite popular in the business world. Major corporations are looking for people to represent their companies online in guiding the blind on the Internet, to selling products through audio and video promotions as well as to guide perspective buyers through sales presentations, and making a company's site both exciting and interactive.

You can set up your own website and offer your imaging services. Include some of your demos for potential clients to listen to. Solicit your clients via e-mail—if you can get your hands on a corporate e-mailing list that would be ideal. You can also become one of the voice talents represented by a website voice imaging casting agent. Go online and type in "website voice imaging" to find agency representation.

Website Voice Imaging Copy

VO Direction: Exuberant read with a moderate to slow pace to accommodate the interactive visuals.

VO: Hello and welcome to Regal Embassy's Educational School Suites demo. Regal Embassy's portable classrooms on wheels provide the perfect solution to overcrowded classrooms in the inner cities across America. This stylish, practical, and spacious learning den was created by Virgil Sly, one of the leading architects in his field. Steve Fagin, writer and chief editor of *School Times* magazine says:

INTERIOR: Close-up of Steve Fagin sitting in a soft velvet chair behind a marble student desk.

Steve Fagin: Regal Embassy has created such a warm and cozy learning environment I want to go back to elementary school again. I highly recommend Educational School Suites!

VO: Well, there you have it, folks. If you live in an area where the kids are in their classrooms packed like sardines in a can, give Regal Embassy a call at 1-800-617-6544, that's 1-800-617-6544, or go to www.regalembassy.com, and let Regal Embassy's Educational School Suites roll into your town and decrease oversized classrooms today!

CHAPTER 5

It's All in the Technique

As defined in *Webster's Dictionary*, technique is a method of accomplishing a certain aim. I struggled for years to hit a golf ball straight down the fairway, but after a series of lessons from a professional, I improved considerably. My talent took me a long way as I plucked the strings of my acoustic guitar, but when a classical virtuoso taught me the proper methods to play the instrument, I reached a level far beyond my expectations.

When you learn the correct way, it makes doing anything easier. When you use the proper techniques to do voice-overs, your efforts will be met with great monetary rewards.

MICROPHONE TECHNIQUES

The way I approach a microphone in a given session is relative to what I am doing in the session. If I'm trying to bring out the low bass qualities in my voice I will get really close—three to four inches is the most effective distance for my full bass sound. If I want to speak louder, I will stand farther back, maybe seven to nine inches, so I don't overload or distort the microphone.

Never feel compelled to shout when you want to project. The microphone is there to make you louder so you don't have to help the process. The microphone should be an extension of you. Your mindset should be: I have my diaphragm, vocal cords, mouth, tongue, lips, voice, and a microphone, now I am ready to perform. When you are one in accord with the microphone, you eliminate the fear of it. You are no longer uptight about stepping up to it. The pressure is off, you can relax.

I think every voice-over actor has a comfort zone in front of the mic, a place where he tends to stand in reference to the mic most of the time. I like to turn my head to the right and work off the right side of the microphone. By working off mic I lessen my chances of popping, which occurs when you blow a burst of air into the mic. The sudden burst causes a sound that generally happens when you use "plosive" words that begin with *t*, *b*, or *p*. Some engineers will put a stocking type device in front of the mic to protect it from plosives. I find this device to be very distracting, which is why I developed my off-mic technique.

The environment in which you record should be lit well enough for you to see your copy clearly and to see the microphone clearly.

I believe the more technique I can provide, the less manipulation and enhancement the engineer has to put on my voice. I prefer the proximity of the microphone to be in a place that doesn't interfere with my reading of the copy. Because I work everything from the right off-axis of the mic, I place my copy on the upper right hand corner of the music stand. With everything in the proper position, I'm able to execute better.

Another very important aspect of microphone technique is lighting. The environment in which you record should be lit well enough for you to see your copy clearly and to see the microphone clearly. If you can't see the mic and you are in real close proximity, you could possibly bump into it, which can be painful and expensive if you damage it.

To be successful, you must let your vocal instrument do all the work. Trust your instrument. When I do dark dramatic trailers like *Clockers* or *Tupac Resurrection*, I hug the mic and let my lower whispery range come through. When I'm doing a comedy trailer like *Friday* or *All About the Benjamins* I stand back from the mic and speak with a smile in my read.

My style of delivery when I speak into the microphone has a lot of air throughout each phrase. Through the years I have perfected this windlike technique to the point where I am in total control of how long or short to make this air sound audible in the microphone.

To become better at using the microphone, you either have to work a lot, practice a lot, or both. If you have good technique, it will enhance your voice-over delivery.

Vocal Exercises

Your vocal cords need exercise to stay in shape. Your diaphragm, which supports your voice, needs exercise. Your lips, your tongue, and the jaw muscles that contort your face and mouth to enunciate and form the vowel sounds to say those multisyllable words need exercise.

I do vocal exercises in my car every day, especially on my way to a voice-over session. One of my favorites is saying "Lips teeth tip of the tongue."

Another favorite is, "Red leather yellow leather." The repetition of these lines at varying speeds is a great vocal workout.

I like to do singing vocalizing, too. I find all of these exercises give me a thorough vocal workout. When I get to my session, I am warmed up and ready to work. You should try a lot of vocal exercises to find out which ones work best for you. Here are some others:

○ Tim told Todd today to take two tiny tablets tomorrow.

○ Black licorice Swiss wristwatch.

○ Better buy the bigger brighter rubber baby buggy bumpers.

○ A proper cup of coffee in a copper coffeepot.

If you have any letter combinations with which you have trouble, make up your own tongue twisters and work on them daily. Sometimes it's hard for me to say the word *remember* when it pops up in some copy, so I composed this little ditty: Remember Randy remember Rosie remember when Rosie met Randy?

Clench your teeth together and repeat this line without taking a breath for as long as you can. I repeat this over and over until the word *remember* flows nice and easy off my lips.

I believe that being physically fit will also make you a better voice-over artist. Your normal cardiovascular exercises will give you the stamina to contend with a day of reading copy in studios. Get in shape! Once you are, it makes breathing properly when you do voice-overs easier.

> **. . . being physically fit will also make you a better voice-over artist.**

You must support your voice from the diaphragm. Your normal stomach exercises like "crunches," are good for strengthening your diaphragm. Breathing is also very important. Here are a few exercises to help you:

○ Inhale and exhale four times slowly through your nose. Your stomach should expand until it's full of the air you just inhaled. Now exhale slowly and gradually pull your stomach in as you exhale. Your stomach should look and feel like it does when you suck in your gut. Repeat. This time inhale and exhale through your mouth.

○ Now add the *ah* sound. Before you start, inhale through your nose, then start the *ah* sound. Hold the note as you exhale. Pull your stomach muscles inward to support the voice as you exhale.

Repeat this exercise again. This time inhale and exhale through your mouth. Remember, when you inhale you take air in. When you exhale you let air out.

○ When you think that you have trained your diaphragm to support your voice, repeat this line as many times as you can in one breath: Harriet Hubbard helps her husband, Henry Hubbard, hose his dirty Chevy down.

If you practice this technique frequently, you'll be breathing correctly when you do voice-overs in no time flat.

Here are a few more tongue twisters. Vary your speed—fast, medium, slow.

○ Peter Piper picked a peck of pretty pickled peppers.

○ Did Peter Piper pick a peck of pretty pickled peppers?

○ If Peter Piper picked a peck of pretty pickled peppers where's the peck of pretty pickled peppers Peter Piper picked?

More tongue twisters, breathing, inflection, and other vocal exercises can be found in Appendix B.

PHRASING—VOCAL EXERCISES

Phrasing can also be used to exercise vocally. We have heard many different versions of our favorite songs performed by different artists. If they all sounded and performed the song exactly the same, how boring would that be? One of the elements that makes one singer's version different from the other is his or her phrasing. The same thing applies to reading copy. We have the ability to phrase it any way we want. We can put a different emphasis on the same sentence every time we read it. Read each sentence below, and put emphasis on the italicized words. The result is a difference in phrasing every time you read the line.

> Did she *say* she loved you?
>
> *Did* she say she loved you?
>
> Did she say she *loved* you?
>
> Did *she* say she loved you?
>
> Did she say she loved *you?*

FIND YOUR OWN VOICE AND WHAT YOU DO BEST

Who are you vocally? Have you ever thought about that? You need to find your own voice. Learn what your sound is, your vocal quality and range. When you define the aspects of your voice that are unique to you, you can develop your own style.

Experienced voice-over performers probably already know. Newcomers need to read a lot of copy from every genre to determine which ones they do best.

I want to present a scenario to you: You are on the telephone with a voice-over casting director with whom you've been trying to make contact for weeks. The conversation might go something like this:

You:	Hi, I'm so glad to finally get to talk with you.
Casting Director:	Great. What can I do for you?
You:	I'd love to read for you sometime.
Casting Director:	Do you have representation?
You:	Yes. I'm with Cunningham.
Casting Director:	Great. Send me your demo.
You:	I was hoping to come in and read.
Casting Director:	What should I have you read, what do you do best?
You:	Anything. I can do it all.

Wrong answer. Nobody can do it all, and you shouldn't try. Don't try to be a voice-over chameleon. We all have our fortés. Versatility is very important but you should stay within your range. Be versatile in what you do best. I'm not saying you can't work in more than one area of voice-over. I'm just suggesting you find the best voice in those areas in which you work the most. If, for instance, you find that employers hire you to do one thing more than others, accept that fact and exploit it. Become even stronger in that. It's okay to work on stretching out to other areas in your spare time, but if you are really taking advantage of your strengths, you'll be so busy working, you probably won't have much spare time to squander aimlessly.

So the next time a casting director asks you what he should have you read if he brings you in, don't say "anything." Pick one or two of your best things. Casting directors are very busy and don't have time to listen to who you want to be vocally, they want to know who you are vocally. If you're just starting out, it won't take long to find out what you're better at. The hard part is being honest about what you're better at. No one is equally good at everything.

Seasoned voice-over performers who are making a great living, stop complaining about being hired almost exclusively to do one kind of voice-over. Be glad you've found your own voice and are being hired regularly. Consider it a blessing.

The Fade

One Monday morning I was sitting in the barber chair for my weekly fade haircut, talking about the Lakers kicking the Clippers in the butt the night before at the Staples Center. Mid-conversation just as I was about to make another point, I felt a jolt in my right side that made me jump. "You got that pager on vibrate again," said my barber, Tank, as he jerked away from my head. "I told you about that thing. I almost cut your ear off, man."

"Hold up, Tank. Let me see who this is," I said as I struggled to get my hands underneath the plastic sheet Tank covers me up with to keep the cut hairs off my clothes. Once I located my pager, I brought it close to my good eye so that I could see who was paging me. Noticing how much I was squinting Tank asked me "You need glasses, man?"

"Yeah, I do," I said as I recognized my agent's number. "Can I use your phone, Tank?"

"Can you see the numbers on this phone?" he joked as he handed me this high-tech phone so small James Bond would have found it too innovative. I had to bring it so close to my face to see the minuscule numbers that he mercifully snatched it away from me and said, "What's the number, man? I'll dial it."

My agent's assistant answered the phone and immediately put me through. With an urgency in his voice my agent spoke loudly, "Rodney, where are you right now?"

"I'm at the barbershop getting my hair cut."

"How fast can you get over to Buzzy's?"

"Well, I'm in North Hollywood and Buzzy's is in West Hollywood on Melrose. How fast do I need to be there?"

"Yesterday. It's a television spot for American Airlines. What time can you be there?"

I looked at the clock on the wall in the barbershop and then at my wristwatch as if it would cause me to answer differently. "I can be there in fifteen minutes." Agents want precision type answers to estimated-time-of-arrival type questions.

"Fifteen minutes, you say. Okay, so it's 9:30 now, so you'll be there by 9:45?" "Yes," I said knowing damn well I couldn't be precise because everything in L.A. depends on the traffic. Agents want to hear positive news because they know that the client wants to hear positive news.

Now to be somewhere in the ballpark of the estimated time of arrival that I gave to my agent, I had to break some very heavy news to Tank. I had to leave immediately. What made this especially hard was the pride that Tank and barbers like him take in their work. They'd rather take a sharp stick in the eye before letting a customer get up out of their chair with a less than a perfect cut. "You gotta what?" Tank hollered as I handed his phone back to him. "I ain't ever heard of nothing like this. I'm almost finished, man." Now see, that's what I'm talking about. He was so far from almost finished, it wasn't even funny. But this is how he and barbers like him operate. Because they are perfectionists, a haircut that should take thirty minutes tops, usually comes in about an hour. Realizing that I was seriously about to vacate the premises and get on the road, and that there was nothing he could do about it, this master of the fade conceded to the inevitable with a caring "Do you have a hat with you, man?"

"No, I don't," I said, "but as soon as I'm finished with the session I'm coming right back okay, Tank?" He didn't say anything; he just sort of stared off into space. Oh my God, I thought as I trotted out of the barbershop, these temperamental artists.

I jumped in my car and took off for Buzzy's. Don't know why, call it vanity maybe, but as soon as I got to Melrose, with just one more block and five minutes left to reach my destination on time, I got the bright idea to look in the mirror at my unfinished haircut. I almost crashed my car. I couldn't believe what I saw. I looked like hell! Well, I told you that fifteen minutes was probably not going to be a reality, but this time I couldn't blame it on L.A. traffic—I had to blame this tardiness on the unfinished fade. I couldn't walk into a studio and be at my best looking like that.

In a panic I drove down Melrose Boulevard looking for a place to buy a hat. I spotted this hip clothing boutique, ran in, and bought a black suede baseball cap. As I drove back down Melrose to Buzzy's already five minutes late I thought, *From now on, this will be my keep-it-in-the-trunk hat, for those rare times that I might have to abruptly leave a haircut in progress.*

CHAPTER 6

Taking Care of Business

N ow, let's take a look at some things that may help you advance your career. You need to keep an eye on your finances— the money that comes in, as well as what goes out. Allot funds exclusively for your trade needs. Secure future work for yourself with unique promotional and marketing strategies. Learn the bylaws of your unions and use them to your advantage in the workplace, especially when it concerns being compensated properly for your labor.

Working from Home, the Home Studio

Technology has made it possible for sessions around the world to be done from the comfort of your home. No longer do you have to be on site. I fought the technology for a long time. I love driving to sessions all day, meeting the clients personally, and eating at some great restaurants along the way, but if you are going to be competitive in your field, you have to pay to play. It became clear to me that I had to spend some money when I found out how much more work I could get done if I invested in this special equipment.

Building the proper environment enhances the quality of your work.

One day I was invited to the home of one of my voice-over buddies. He showed me his home studio and how the different pieces of gear worked. I'm not a very technical person, which was another reason that I never really considered a studio, but when he demonstrated how easy it was to use this stuff, I immediately asked for a pen and paper and proceeded to write down the names of everything in the place. I even asked him for the name of the contractor who built his studio. I was so impressed I wanted to copy his place to a tee.

I went home and went to work. The first thing I did was purchase a Telos Zephyr Express. This is a remarkable machine. It's portable so you can take it on vacation and do voice-overs from your hotel room. This is ideal for an occupation that works 24/7. When I declare a vacation period, the hundreds of thousands of dollars available don't stop being distributed. If my agent calls me with an extremely lucrative opportunity, with the portable Telos Zephyr I have the option of taking the job or not. It combines a flexible stereo digital mixer, two stereo monitor mixers, and inputs for your microphone and headphones.

The next thing I had to do was figure out what part of my home I wanted to use to construct a voice-over booth. After deciding where it should go, I called the builder, he took some measurements, and we set a start date. With his three-man crew he finished my booth in one weekend. I called the telephone company and had an ISDN (International Standard Digital Network) line installed for digital connections.

Now in plain English, here is what I do: I turn the Telos Zephyr on, the client in, let's say, New York, dials me up, and voilà! The session begins. I hear her through my headphones and she hears me when I speak into the microphone. More importantly the digital connection makes it sound just like I'm there. I have voiced many trailers like *Bamboozled*, *Finding Forrester*, and *Friday After Next* via ISDN right from my home.

Selecting a microphone was an easy decision because I decided to use the industry standard. In most of the studios in which I've worked around the Los Angeles area, the 416 Sennheiser is used, so I bought it.

My headphones are another industry standard, the Sony Professionals. That's it! The microphone, the headphones, and the ISDN line are all connected to the Telos Zephyr. I still prefer to drive to the studios, but the convenience of the ISDN line cannot be denied. I use it most often in the early mornings to accommodate my east coast sessions, and in the evenings after-hours.

I am also capable of producing finished spots for my clients with the use of my editing software, Sonic Foundry Sound Forge 6.0. I can e-mail these spots to the client in the form of MP3, WAVE, or AIFF files with my PCV-RX650 Sony VAIO Digital Studio Computer. Clients can also retrieve the spots from my website or download them from my FTP site, a file transfer system.

Recently I was the guest speaker at a voice-over seminar and was asked the following questions about the home studio. Perhaps you have some of the same concerns:

- ○ **At what point in your career should you consider building a home studio?** When you can afford it, and when you have committed to pursuing a career in voice-overs.

- ○ **Is the studio supposed to be soundproof?** It would be best; however if you can't afford to build a soundproof booth, just find a quiet environment to record in. Closets are great because of the hanging clothes that deaden the room. Be creative. Any quiet space will do.

○ **Do you have to buy all of the components mentioned or can you get away with one or two pieces?** It depends on what you are trying to accomplish. If you only want to record and send your voice out over the Internet, then all you need is a computer, mixing board, and a microphone. Generally, it would be better to have every component up and running at full capacity. The costs are less than $10,000 for everything that I have mentioned.

○ **Is building a studio a good choice for someone who doesn't want to move to New York or L.A.?** Absolutely. New York and Los Angeles are the entertainment capitals of the world. The majority of voice-over work is produced in these locations. With a home studio equipped with ISDN capabilities you are virtually there. Some of the top voice-over talents in the country live outside of these major markets. The reality is you can be anywhere and still be in the game.

MONEY

The question I am asked most often when someone finds out I do voice-overs is how much money can you make. It's potentially a very lucrative career, which has made a lot of talented people very rich. Many voice-over actors right here in Los Angeles are enjoying healthy six-figure annual salaries. Some have even reached seven-figures-a-year status.

The figures that follow are subject to change due to union pay raises and what your agent or representative is able to negotiate for you. For instance, where I specify a union scale, some talent may get double scale for that particular job because their stature in the industry demands it. Where I specify general ranges in salary, some performers may get more than the average top range.

You should always check with your local SAG and AFTRA union to see what the current scale rates are for any job you work on. Television rates differ from radio and cable rates. Check with the union for those differences.

Also keep in mind that a lot of these categories can produce huge amounts of residual monies. I've listed some categories that don't fall under any union jurisdiction and are purely negotiable fields that usually pay somewhere in the neighborhood of the prices I have listed. With that in mind, here are a few numbers:

Animation—Union scale is $678 per day

Trailers—$1000 to $2,200 per trailer

Television Promo—Union scale is $220 per spot

Television Tag—$93 per tag

Radio Promo—$220 per spot

Radio Tag—$91 per tag

Trailer Tag—$250 to $370 per tag

Audiobooks—$2,500 to $4,000 per book

Commercials—Union scale is $400 per spot (California rate)

Industrial Narrations—$1,500 and up per industrial

Demos—Usually half of whatever the negotiated salary is for the finished job

Voice Matches (Sound-Alikes)—Union scale is $678 per match

Interstitials (Short Takes)—$1,500 and up per session

EPK (Electronic Press Kit)—$1,500 and up

Narration—first hour $346; each additional half hour $101

Narrator Spokesperson—$769 per day; each additional day $423

ADR Walla-Looping—$678 per session

Voice Prompts—$200 per session

Radio Imaging—$200 to $300 monthly (negotiable)

Live Announce—Union scale is $678 (more is usually negotiated)

These are just some of the many ways to make money in voice-overs. At first glance of this list, one might say, "Where is the big money?" Well, when you consider the fact that a successful voice-over artist does one or two or all of the above categories several times a day then collects residuals (money) on many of these jobs monthly and for years later, you start to understand and appreciate the money.

Make Money While You Sleep

Residuals are the fruit of a voice-over actor's labor. You get residuals every time one of your voice-over commercials plays on network, basic cable, and pay TV. You also get residuals when your work is sold on videocassettes and DVDs or played on foreign pay TV or national radio. If you are lucky enough to be the signature voice of a particular product, one long-running national spot could pay as much as a hundred thousand dollars in residuals.

Don't be discouraged if you don't personally see or hear your commercials. The checks you receive in the mail are a good reminder that even though you keep missing them, your commercials are running in various markets across the country every minute of the day.

If by chance you don't see your commercial because it really isn't on the air anymore, all is not lost if you receive a holding fee check, which comes from the advertising agency that produced your commercial and wants to hold you (your voice in the spot) but not run the spot. You will receive a holding fee every thirteen weeks until the agency decides to run the spot again or drop it. If they drop the spot, they will send your agent a letter informing her that you have been released.

Residuals alone are a good reason to be in the union. Generally, you cannot collect residuals for non-union work.

Keep Good Records and Follow Your Money

Freelance work tends to make employers think that they are getting the talents' services for free. The loose structure inherent in the word often eliminates the courtesy of paying talent in a timely fashion, or even paying them at all. Yes, we do have unions that levy fines and late fees on these employers for their conduct, but we as individuals have to take the ball into our on hands and "mind our own business."

I always keep very thorough records of all the work I do. When you work on a job, the employer will give you the performer's copy of the contract you sign. More often than not the performer's copy is the very last of two to three pages that is barely legible. I politely ask for a photocopy of the first page on the contract, plus the carbon performer's copy.

This very legible white copy leaves no doubt about the information on the contract. To make sure you are paid the negotiated amount each cycle that your commercial is used, you should always remember to write "per spot/per cycle" next to the rate on the original contract. This makes it contractually binding to pay you the negotiated fee every thirteen weeks the commercial runs. To make sure your agent's compensation is not taken out of your payment write, "plus ten percent" beside your negotiated rate. Not only should you keep a copy of each session contract, you should make copies for your agent and the accountant at your agency who processes your checks.

Send a copy of the contract to the union within twenty-four hours after the session. A late delivery of your contract to the union may result in them fining you. You can never have too many copies of your contracts distributed to the proper personnel. When you have a discrepancy about your contract, you want everybody who can support your cause to have a copy.

Hoard every contract from any and every job. You may have to go back two years or more to make a claim for monies owed to you. The original contract could prove essential and beneficial to your claim. I have made thousands of "back" dollars because I kept the contracts for promos and commercials that were "reused" without compensating me. I even go one step farther by keeping the scripts from each session I work on—more ammunition to support my potential claims.

Never assume that a contract will be presented to you before or after a session. To be sure that one is available, keep contracts from each union and jurisdiction with you at all times. Remember, there is no better way to make sure you are paid than a signed and dated contract. Be extra nice to all of those diligent people who help you collect your money, but never be content with their effort alone. No one wants you to have your money more than you do!

Your friends around the country can also be great watch dogs for you. Encourage them to let you know when they think they have heard you on television, radio, or the Internet.

Never throw your pay stubs away. Your accountant will love you for this one as well as future bank institutions who are considering loaning you money. They need your check stubs to verify your income. Freelance artists have to jump through more hoops than a trained seal to get mortgage loans, car loans, etc. Good records will make the loan process a lot easier.

At the beginning of each calendar year, you should have an appointment book so that you can record each job you work on. I always draw a box on the page of the date I do my session. Inside the box I write down the name of the product, how many spots I did, the name of the production company, the time of the session, and where the session took place. Pick up one of those red ink stamps that reads "paid," from your nearest office supply store. When you receive payment stamp in the box. This enables you to know who does and who doesn't owe you money.

Keep a ledger. If you know how much money you make each month, you will work harder the following month if you didn't meet your expectations the month before. You can't exercise this motivational tool if you don't keep a ledger and record your income.

Keep good records and follow your money.

What to Do with Your Money

Ultimately, what you do with your money is your business. I just want to impart some advice that was given to me by some voice-over heavyweights when I became successful in this business and started making substantial money.

○ **Pay yourself first.** Believe me, if you open an account at the bank and put ten percent of your net income from every check you receive into that account, you will gain much wealth fast! This is a form of saving that will give you financial independence quicker than any other plan I know.

○ **Put some money back into your career.** You have to pay to play. You must update your demos. As soon as you are financially able, you should buy the latest technology to keep up with your competitors. Invest in a home studio. For less than $10,000 you can have your own studio at home. The industry is changing fast every day. People all over the country need voice-over talent. It's a classic case of supply and demand. With Internet access and the equipment I am urging you to buy, you can supply the voice for that countrywide demand.

○ **Compartmentalize.** You want to make a demo tape? Open a savings or checking account and start saving for your voice-over CD demo. You want a home studio or some expensive new editing software? How about a brand-new high-end microphone? You can buy all of these things in a short time if you have a designated account that facilitates your voice-over professional needs. Contribute weekly to your voice-over account and your home studio will be up and running in no time.

Promote Yourself–Marketing Strategies

While it's true that voice-over talent is expected to be heard and not seen, when it comes to securing steady work, your mission should always be to make sure the right people know who you are. The voice-over business is a high-stakes, competitive industry and there is no time to be modest when it comes to letting potential clients know you are the person for their next project. Here are a few strategies that can help you stay on top of your game:

Gorilla Marketing is when you come down on your clients, old and new, like torrential rains. Never let them forget who you are and what you are capable of doing for them. There is no such thing as overkill in the voice-over business. The more you put yourself in clients' minds, the better your chances for employment. Be aggressive. Don't be afraid to cold call, but make sure it's at the right time. Producers tend to pick up their direct lines at the end of the day or early in the morning.

Prepare your pitch before you make your call. If you happen to catch the top dog, you'd better have a message to deliver. Your agent responds to incoming calls, seldom does she make calls on your behalf. You have to make those calls yourself.

Get to know the assistants of the producers with whom you are trying to make contact. A good telephone relationship with the assistant of a major producer will definitely increase your chances of making contact with that producer. Take the time to compile a list of important calls that you need to make. Don't spin your wheels for nothing; make sure the people you call have the power to deliver.

The Saturation Method happens when you flood the market with your product, which is you. Sending your demos, postcards, and newsletters to as many potential employers as possible. What you have to offer is no different than what Coca Cola, American Express, or General Motors offers. What do they do? They advertise over and over and over until you can't help but purchase the product they've saturated you with. You're going to turn off a few, just like advertisers do, but the numbers you will reach with the saturation method will guarantee you some measure of success.

Postcards are excellent marketing tools because the stamps are inexpensive. The small size makes them cheaper to print and produce in bulk. You can send them out daily, weekly, or monthly. The contents on the card can be as simple as just your name and agent contact information. More elaborate cards may have your picture and a small list of credits. The idea here is to get your name on the client's brain.

Newsletters work great for clients with whom you've worked before. As crazy as it may sound to think that someone would want to read about what is going on in your professional life, you'd be surprised at how much employers really find this information valuable and enjoyable. The newsletter should talk about recent jobs and upcoming places your voice can be heard. Employers want to hire who they believe everyone else is hiring, so the newsletter will let them know everyone else is hiring you.

New Demos are another opportunity to do mass mailings. Whenever you do a job, ask the production company to give you a copy of the finished spot. Sometimes they will request money. If they do, gladly pay them. I wouldn't pay any more than twenty-five dollars. Add the new element in an edited version to your demo and make duplicate copies from your master. Now you are ready to send them off. A letter urging everyone to listen to your new demo should be included in the package.

Holiday Cards will benefit you in a couple of ways. First, sending a greeting to employers is a very kind gesture that suggests that you care about their happiness and well-being on a level that exceeds your professional relationship with them. Second, it also gets your name out there. Do not send Christmas or Hanukkah cards. So many times we think we know the religious practices and beliefs of a certain individual, only to discover later that we were wrong. To avoid possibly offending someone, send out cards that simply state, "Happy Holidays."

Brand Name your career. Establish a presence in the market that makes anything you do recognizable. When you send out postcards and demos, stamp each item with your own unique logo. Make T-shirts, mugs, or ink pens with your name and logo on them. Every selling point that applies to the largest corporations in the world applies to you. You have to act like a corporation.

Special Mailing Campaigns. Whenever you do a television or radio commercial, promo, or trailer campaign, get a copy of the audio portion of the spot and make about fifty CD copies of it. The CD labels should have the name of the product on the top and your name listed as the VO talent on the bottom. Search magazines or other periodicals for a picture of the product. If you can find one, make fifty copies of the picture. If you are not successful in your search, don't worry about it, it's not essential. Compose a letter that talks about you being the voice-over talent for the product, and make fifty copies of it. Compile a list of the fifty most influential producers and directors to whom to send this package. Every time you do a significant campaign that will play on a consistent rotation on television or radio for at least one week, you can repeat this process.

Be Your Own Brand Name by David McNally and Karl D. Speak is a great book for learning more about establishing your brand name.

On a postcard you can promote a new commercial, an audiobook narration, or, animation job. Be creative. I recommend a glossy finish on the front side of the card

Sample Newsletter

VALLEY EDITION

PILLSBURY NEWS

IN JUST ONE SHORT WEEK YOU WILL
RECEIVE THE LONG AWAITED, HIGHLY
ANTICIPATED, MUCH APPRECIATED

TRESLYN PILLSBURY
PROMO DEMO

Featuring Promos From:
  ATC Daytime Television
  RTPN Sports
  NCC Thursday Nightly Line-up
  Country Western Oleo Awards

Treslyn delivers! And in just one week this promo
CD will be yours! For bookings and auditions contact The Baldwin Agency: 818-568-5234

**Treslyn is also the voice of "Mrs. Bailey"
on BEX's new animated television series
PREPPY TEENS.**

Sample Postcard–Front

PRESENTING
RICHARD DRYSDALE
AS THE TV TRAILER AND RADIO CAMPAIGN
VOICE
FOR

URBAN FEVER

Back

YOUR CONTACT INFORMATION
**For bookings and
auditions contact
Peter Hayes of MTA
at (310) 555-6734
For further information
or a demo tape, contact
Karen Ann Tripp of
Tripp Management
(818) 555-3315**

**Name
& Address
of Producer**

for a more eye-catching and professional look. Colors are also recommended but more expensive.

NEVER BE UNEMPLOYED AGAIN

There is no good reason in the world for you not to be a busy voice-over artist. So many times when I have conversations with other voice-over talent, I hear them complaining about the scarcity of work, and they don't believe the future will be any better for them. They accept their unemployment and wear it as a badge of honor. "You know how it is, things are slow right now," they say or, "That's just how it is in the voice-over business." What a defeatist attitude.

> **It is not always the most talented VO actor who wins the race, but the one who never stops running. Persistence is the key to success.**

Did you know that thoughts are things? If you believe and think that you won't work, you know what? You won't. You should never accept unemployment. You should never be unemployed. There is always work to do. When you're not working you should be working on getting work. There is no time for rest. The payment for working is not always someone handing you a paycheck. When you are so-called unemployed, you really are "employed," if you are actively pursuing work. Your "payment" is the seeds you have planted in your pursuit of monetary compensation. So you see, you are never really out of work. Your job is really not that hard when you think about it, the only person you have to get work for is you.

My success is based solely on my attitude and drive. Sure, I've been told that I have talent and that I'm good at what I do, but I don't rest on those complimentary laurels. I work because I believe I'm supposed to work, and when I invite that positive current into my life, abundance finds me. A positive attitude makes me easy to find.

A long time ago I started thinking about how the companies that hire me have a number of full-time employees who work for them. These employees have children to support, mortgages to pay, yet these production companies manage to employ and insure all of these people and their families. I thought, If that company can employ and pay a large group of people, why can't I support just me? *Why should I ever be out of work or broke?* That concept alone changed my whole professional life.

If you come from the place of believing that someone is always in need of a voice-over, someone will always be in need of a voice-over. People are always in need of insurance, groceries, or a plumber. Why wouldn't they be in need of you?

Producers just need to know you are out there when they have a need. This brings us back to the fact that you have to become a brand name. I guarantee you that once you establish yourself in the marketplace, there is no way that you can be ignored. Whether or not you become Wal-Mart or just a mom-and-pop store remains to be seen, but you will be one or the other, or something in between when you make your availability known to those seeking a voice-over.

Don't sweat the downtime worrying about it being "downtime," sweat working and creating ways to minimize future downtimes. When Sears reports a down quarter, do they stop working, send all their employees home, and bow their heads? No, they work harder to meet or surpass the next quarter's expectations. In other words, work on new ideas to promote yourself. I can't stress enough how important it is for you to align yourself with and think like a big corporation.

Practice some dialects that you may not be that good at and even harder on the ones you are good at. Take a voice-over class. Always be working! My motto is "work hard to play hard." The harder I work at working, the more work I get, which makes my vacations that much sweeter. You can't beat hard work. You can't beat beating your competition to the punch. It won't be hard because most people are lazy. Your competition for the most part will be sitting around waiting on their agents and managers to get work for them. I found out a long time ago, there's not a whole lot of traffic in the hard work lane. You have to change the way you perceive yourself and never be unemployed again!

Vanity Plates

Los Angeles is known for its Hollywood glamour. From the celebrities to the mansions in Beverly Hills, this place brings out the gaudiness in all of us. No matter how low-key or introverted you may have been before you moved to California, when you've been here for a while, you find that the extrovert in you comes to the surface.

My gaudy nature surfaced when I started to notice and admire the vanity license plates as I drove around the city. It was fun to try and translate them. Once I figured out what the plate said, it was important for me to see the person who came up with such a clever plate, so I would try to get alongside of her and catch a peek at her face. If I was lucky enough to sit at a long red light right beside the person, I could really examine her face while thinking, *What kind of person are you that would make you have a vanity plate like that?*

One day I got the bright idea to get my own vanity plates. I sat up for long hours through the night trying to come up with that perfect one. Every time I came up with something I liked, I would call the Department of Motor Vehicles to register the name only to be told it was already taken. I juggled this letter with that, replaced this number with another, and the DMV finally let me register my own cryptic creation. And what fancy dandy of a name did I come up with? A1VOICE. Hey, it made sense to me. I was a voice-over artist by profession, and I considered my skills to be A1, like the steak sauce. As far as I was concerned this was a pretty cool license plate, and the people who mattered most in my life agreed.

When I received my plates in the mail, I slapped them on my car as fast as I could and hit the road. Maybe it was all in my mind but I felt like everybody I passed or who passed me that first day, acknowledged my plates in some form or fashion. I found people staring into the windows of my car at stoplights just like I used to do. Some would just stare; others would smile and give me the okay sign.

I spent a couple of years or so with those plates and soon they were starting to take their toll on the introverted side of my personality. Such recognizable plates always let people know my whereabouts. Often people would say to me, "I saw your car out in front of the store," or "I saw you driving down the street." One time, while my mother was visiting me from Detroit, we were having breakfast at one of her favorite haunts, Roscoe's Chicken & Waffles, when these two fine sisters came into the small eatery and one of them shouted out, "Who is A1VOICE?" My proud mother looked at me, and I sheepishly said "Me." Constantly at car washes, gas stations, and stoplights, I would be asked to explain the meaning of my plates.

One of the reasons that the voice-over field was so perfect for me was its anonymity factor. It was the behind-the-scenes and out-of-the-limelight nature of a voice-over career that really appealed to me. I was beginning to become uncomfortable with this brazen act of advertising to strangers what I did for a living. I was also noticing a certain maturity coming into my life that made me even more *inside* the more successful I got. The richer I became monetarily from the business, the less I wanted anyone to know about it. It was looking like a sure bet that I would not renew those plates, when something occurred in my life that finally pushed me over the top.

I parked my Benz on Wilshire Boulevard in Beverly Hills. I got out of the car, pulled a couple of quarters out of my pocket, and put them in the parking meter. Then I turned around to walk into the building when I noticed the greatest session keyboard player in the music business coming up the street. I revered this guy as a musician. If you wanted the best, he was the man to call. I've followed his career from the late seventies in Detroit where I first saw him playing with Stevie Wonder to his more recent success. He has worked with Michael Jackson, Quincy Jones, Lionel Richie, and Eric Clapton. Any heavyweight you can name, male or female, this guy has worked with them. And now was my chance to meet him. I pulled out another quarter to put in the meter just to stall myself long enough for him to reach me.

"Hello," I said as I extended my hand. "I'm Rodney Saulsberry." He didn't know me from Adam but he was receptive to my approaching him. "I really enjoy your work, brother," I told him.

"Thank you," he said. Looking down at my license plate he asked me, "What do you do?" Now I was thinking this is really cool. Someone I thought so much of was interested in what I did for a living. I couldn't wait to spill the beans. With a smile stretched so wide that it still pains my jaw muscles today when I think about it, I said, "I do voice-overs."

He looked back down at my license plate, and with the deadpan calm of a first chair concert cellist he said, "And you want everybody to know it." I don't recall what else was said in that brief encounter after he dropped that bomb on me, but on the following day, I made arrangements to get new non-vanity license plates, and I have never regretted that decision.

CHAPTER 7

Staying On Top of It All

O nce you reach the pinnacle of success in your mind, the key is to stay there. Keeping the career on an upward path should be your primary goal. To do this you need to make sure your agent is still working hard for you. If he isn't, you might be better off seeking new representation. You need to be in control of your destiny, and you need to address your physical well-being as well as your mental outlook.

CHANGING AGENCIES–HOW TO MAKE A SMOOTH TRANSITION

When you move from one agency to another the first thing you want to do is spread the news to the voice-over community about your new representation. There are many ways to do this:

○ **Do mass mailings.** Hopefully your new agency will assist you by doing this to all of their clients, informing them of your arrival. You should also do this personally every three or four months since it takes casting directors about a year to get use to your new location.

○ **Make a new demo.** You'll have to change the agency name on your CD anyway, so why not change its content as well and get a fresh start.

○ **Inform the unions.** This is important so that your future payments and residuals are sure to reach you. Ask the accounting department at your former agency for a copy of all of your current commercials running and any upcoming renegotiations. Most will be glad to give you that information. If you encounter any problems acquiring these documents, ask your union to request them for you.

○ **Call old employers.** Taking the time to personally contact people with whom you've had a friendly relationship adds a nice personal touch.

When I moved to my new agency, it was amazing to me how supportive the voice-over community was about

Sample New Agency Representation Newsletter

This announcement works for beginners as well as seasoned voice actors who want to inform the industry of their new representation.

**** IMPORTANT ANNOUNCEMENT ****

WE ARE PLEASED TO ADVISE THAT
EFFECTIVE IMMEDIATELY

COMMERCIAL/ANIMATION
VOICE-OVER TALENT

STEVEN HOGANBART

IS NOW EXCLUSIVE WITH THE
DRUMMOND PETE VOICE-OVER AGENCY

TO BOOK OR AUDITION STEVEN,
PLEASE CALL

Mark Knott
DRUMMOND PETE VOICE-OVER AGENCY
Phone: 310-555-6834
Fax: 310-555-6709

WE LOOK FORWARD TO HEARING FROM YOU!

---

my move. The way the industry operates, as long as you're happy, they're happy. They just wanted to know where I was so they could find me when they wanted to hire me.

I signed with the William Morris Agency in the summer of 2002 and started booking jobs within the first few days of my signing. I never missed a beat, and I reached even higher heights in my voice-over career.

HOW TO BE IN CONTROL OF YOUR VOICE-OVER DESTINY

Let me share some of the reasons why the top money-makers in the voice-over industry are at the top, and thus control their voice-over destinies. They will be successful for many years to come because:

- ○ **They think they're supposed to be.** What you think about, you bring about.

- ○ **They have focus.** Wear blinders as you race to the target that is success.

- ○ **They take care of their instrument.** Treat your voice well.

- ○ **They have a plan.** Define your goal, and then decide on a course of action.

- ○ **They have no fear of failure.** You might not make it, but do dare to try.

- ○ **They have extreme confidence.** Believe that no matter what, you will prevail.

○ **They practice.** Your habitual practicing makes being excellent a habit.

○ **They are punctual.** On time beats being late every time.

○ **They are professional.** Conduct yourself in a businesslike manner in and out of the studio.

○ **They have direction.** Your positive direction gets you where you want to be.

○ **They know who they are.** You have to find the "money voice" in you.

○ **They have omnipotence.** Achieve unlimited "power" in your attitude.

○ **They hunger for knowledge.** You're always a student. Take more VO classes.

○ **They adjust to change.** Be aware of changes in the voice-over industry.

If you strive to possess all of the attributes above, you, too, will be in control of your voice-over destiny and be successful for many years to come.

You Absolutely Cannot Afford to Catch a Cold!

You must take care of yourself. God forbid you should miss out on thousands of dollars because of the common cold. I don't care if you have to put your sick loved ones in quarantine so you are not infected, you cannot catch a cold! Okay, seriously, I know it's impossible for anyone to completely avoid catching a cold, but you must maintain a working vocal instrument through it all.

Knock on wood, I have never missed a job due to sickness. Yes, I have been sick and felt very bad many times, but I've always managed to do the job. My sickness went undetected. My employers never knew I was not at my best. I pulled it off.

Never reveal feeling ill. As soon as you feel a cold coming on, take action.

When you're under the weather and you come to a session, greet your employers normally. When they ask you how you're doing, you should tell them that you're doing fine. Remember, if you tell them that you're hoarse, or that your nasal passages are stuffed, believe me they will hear those hoarse vocal cords and clogged up nostrils on every take. Never reveal feeling ill. As soon as you feel a cold coming on, take action.

There are many things you can do to either beat it completely or maintain it while you still work. There is no substitute for rest. When I refer to rest, I'm not talking about sleeping; I'm talking about shutting up. In my Broadway musical days, the one thing I learned from the older singers was to be quiet when I wasn't working. We did eight shows a week. In-between time had to be our rest time if we were going to be great for every performance.

Family and friends will find your being "quiet" very difficult to deal with, but you must impress upon them that your voice is your livelihood.

I am not a doctor but these things have worked for me when I'm feeling sick:

- Gargle with a small cup of salt water before you go to bed. Drink plenty of room-temperature water.

- Drink hot green tea with two teaspoons of honey to soothe and coat the throat as much as needed.

- Sleep with a humidifier to avoid dry air in the room.

- Find your favorite cough drop or throat lozenge to give you relief when you feel soreness. Always keep the one that soothes you best on hand.

- Eating some food (nothing dairy) tends to be good for the vocal cords. I find that food coats my throat and also makes my stomach happy.

- Adrenaline will also be your friend when your voice is not at its best. When you step up to the microphone your adrenaline will give you surprising vocal strength.

- Nervous energy will work in your favor, too.

Your mental state has to be positive. You have to believe you can perform under this temporary duress. A positive attitude together with some of these tips I have provided should get the job done.

Fortunately, I have never had laryngitis. I've been told that with it, sometimes you lose your voice completely. Obviously you can't work in that condition. You should check with an ear, nose, and throat doctor if you suffer laryngitis-like symptoms. Your voice is your franchise.

SOME COMMON MISTAKES TO AVOID

You have the opportunity by reading this book to avoid making some of the common mistakes many people have made in this business. If you have already made some of them, it's not the end of the world. Just try not to make them again.

In my opinion, the most common mistake made by people trying to break into the voice-over business is an unprofessional presentation, like unattractive business cards, postcards, and CD cover graphics. Here are a few more:

○ **Poorly recorded demo tapes.** Distorted, inaudible demos are unacceptable and unprofessional. A low-quality presentation of this sort suggests a cavalier attitude about your career. You have to spend the money for a top-notch engineer and recording studio if you want to compete in the business. I can't stress it enough: The demo is the most important tool in your voice-over arsenal.

○ **Limited marketing.** Once you have an agent, you need to flood the market with your demo. If you don't, you limit your chances of visibility in the marketplace. You need 150 to 200 demos to be effective. Don't send them all out at once—schedule your mailings. Four mailings a year is sufficient.

Use common sense when sending thank-you cards and making follow-up calls. Not everyone is receptive to either. Use your best judgment.

○ **Expecting overnight success.** It doesn't normally happen that way. Learn the business. You can't expect to flourish in something you don't know about. Familiarize yourself with the craft. Pay your dues.

○ **No experience.** If you don't have any experience, you have to take voice-over and acting classes before you attempt to do voice-overs.

○ **No commitment.** People who don't jump in with both feet are not committed. You have to give this business your undivided attention.

- **Having a bad attitude.** Don't be negative; you have to believe you can be successful.

- **Settling for less.** Don't take the first agent who wants to represent you. Make sure that this is the right fit for you. You may end up accepting the first offer, but do see some other agents before signing a contract.

- **Throwing in the towel.** Don't give up. Be patient. Remember, anything really worthwhile is worth waiting for.

- **Allowing your agent to take upfront money.** Never give money to your agent or anybody he tells you to give money to. If a request of this nature is ever made, you should leave that agent immediately. An agent takes a ten percent commission from any work he gets. That's it.

- **Overpaying for services.** Don't overpay. Make sure you do your research and compare prices. Ask friends and colleagues in the business for reputable quality at reasonable rates.

- **Not socializing.** Beginners have to socialize. It's a great way to promote yourself. If you attend voice-over parties and other social functions, you'll meet people who might be able to assist you in getting work.

- **Bad hygiene.** You are in constant contact with people in the workplace. Do yourself and your colleagues a favor by staying fresh of body and breath at all times. Keep in mind, some people don't like too much perfume or cologne.

○ **Not following up.** When you work for a new client, send a thank-you card. When you send your demo to a casting director, make a follow-up call to make sure he received it.

○ **Insufficient sleep.** A tired voice-over artist is a soon-to-be unemployed voice-over artist. If you don't get your sleep, you can't be in top form. You must rest. It is absolutely mandatory!

RODNEY'S TEN VOICE-OVER CREEDS TO LIVE BY

○ Get to your auditions early and your sessions even earlier.

○ Have tunnel vision at your auditions.

○ Warm up before every job.

○ Visualize your voice-over success.

○ Act like a professional if you want to be treated like a professional.

○ Sign and keep track of all your contracts, forever!

○ Practice, practice, practice.

○ Market yourself constantly.

○ Believe in yourself.

○ Do something each day to advance your career.

THE LIVE ANNOUNCE

As far as I'm concerned, there is nothing in the business of voice-over that presents more on-the-job pressure than being the announcer for a two-hour nationally televised special in front of a live audience. If you're fortunate enough to get a couple of rehearsals in before the show, you'll be lucky. Unfortunately, time restraints usually make more than one run-through impossible.

When the announcer arrives at the venue, he receives a very large ring binder with the entire show in it. Every page is numbered. The numbers will stay the same, but the content on a particular page can change constantly— right up to the live show and during the live show. The writers and producers change the script minutes before an event and the announcer gets these changes from the script supervisor and has to rip out the old pages and replace them with the new ones.

Sitting or standing at a podium backstage in a reserved room somewhere in the theater or outside the venue in a technical crew truck, the announcer should be in deep concentration as he listens intently for direction from the assistant director through his headphones. The announcer listens intently because it's not easy to hear your direction when you can also hear the director directing the entire show in your headphones. Each camera operator, the sound guys, the musical director, and the lighting crew are all being told what to do simultaneously, and you have to listen for your cues through all the madness. The key to being successful in this format is complete concentration at all times.

The first thing to do is familiarize yourself with the proper pronunciations of all the names you will have to announce. Hopefully, your producer will supply you with a list of phonetic spellings. Chances are twenty to fifty percent of the show will change before the live one, but you should study the present script as much as possible anyway during breaks.

A conversation with the producers about the tone of the show, how up or down your reads (energy) should be should occur at some point soon after you receive your script. In some cases, you should also be prepared to be your own engineer. That's right, you control the sending of your voice to the television audience in the theater and around the world by pushing a button every time the director cues you to announce. The device that houses this very important button is called a talkback box. Just one more thing to concentrate on.

When I did my first live announce for the *34th NAACP Image Awards* on March 8, 2003, from the Universal Amphitheatre in Universal City, California, it was new territory for me. I had never done that type of work before, and furthermore, I had always stated that I would never do it.

Never say never. Given the opportunity, I jumped at the chance. I was hired about a week before the show, so I had little time to prepare for this new challenge. I didn't get the script in advance, so I had nothing to study. I made calls to some of my announcer friends who had done live announces before and took extensive notes from them. I went on the Internet and read out loud legal copy, rules, and regulations about how winners were chosen from the *Oscars*, the *Grammys*, the *Emmys*, and past *NAACP Image Award* shows. There was even an Image Award website for the upcoming 2003 show that listed the name of the host and all the guests who would be on the show. I must have read it out loud at least a thousand times: "From the Universal Amphitheatre in Los Angeles, Welcome to the *34th NAACP Image Awards*." My biggest fear was that I would say "Welcome to the 34th NCAA (National Collegiate Athletic Association) Image Awards."

My call time to the theater was 11:30 A.M. As usual I was very early. One of the staff members took me to the backstage area where all of the administrative business was going on. There were about a hundred and twenty-five men and women in black T-shirts with backstage credentials around their necks, running around. I was introduced to all of the people with whom I would be working, given my backstage credentials, and handed a very heavy, humongous binder that contained the entire show. Now remember, I didn't know what was coming next. I was flying by the seat of my pants, but acting as if I was an old pro.

I was taken to what would be my vocal booth, a dressing room. This wasn't just any dressing room. On one side of me was a two-time Oscar winner, down the hall was one of my favorite directors, and to completely interrupt my concentration, just knowing that the most beautiful actress in the world in my opinion was in the vicinity made my vocal cords tight.

There was a man in my dressing room-turned-vocal booth who I assumed would be my engineer. On a long table in the middle of the room was everything I would need to do my job. I was familiar with the television monitor that gave me the ability to watch the show as I announced, a set of headphones, a microphone, and a mixing board, but I didn't recognize the black box with about four buttons on it that I was later told was a talk-back box.

The man started to instruct me on how to operate it. I listened half-heartedly because I assumed he would be controlling all the contraptions before me.

After his tutorial he got up to leave.

"Aren't you staying?" I asked.

"No," he replied.

"Am I supposed to work this talkback box?" I asked.

"Most of the announcers do. If you need me to stay, I will," he said with all of the insincerity he could muster.

"Oh no, I can handle it," I said.

The run-through was very educational. I learned everything I needed to know during those two hours, and most of all, I learned that I was terrified about the thought of the live show. My biggest fear was still those opening lines. I kept thinking about how I would be the first voice the audience heard at the top of the show. That thought alone caused me to eat nothing during our dinner break. I didn't think I could keep any food down. My diet from the time I arrived at the theater was water. I used the dinner break to go over my script. I was just starting to get comfortable with it when this man came into the room and handed me a script revision packet. Notice the word *packet*, which means a lot of pages. All day long I had been given a few pink pages or a couple of tan revised pages, but this was a whole bunch of pages. So much for my dinnertime studies, I had to spend the rest of the hour replacing pages.

I brought a change of clothes to wear during the show. Not a tux or anything like that, just some nice black slacks and a black short-sleeved mock turtleneck. I wanted to delineate in my mind the difference between rehearsal and the real thing.

The clock was moving fast toward the start of the show. New revisions were still coming my way. Some notes from the producer about my performance in the rehearsal were delivered to me, and I was ready to rock when in walked one of the female celebrity presenters and her entourage of five to do a prerecord ten minutes before curtain. And I was expected to engineer the recording. Problem was, the man who taught me how to use the talkback box didn't tell me how to record some-one, and he was nowhere to be found. As we all looked around helplessly, I noticed that in exactly one minute I had to introduce the opening of the show. Scrambling to sit down in front of the microphone, I accidentally knocked my script to the floor. Luckily the rings in the binder were closed and I didn't get the pages out of order. As I picked up the script, another thought infiltrated my mind: the celebrity presenter and company were not leaving. This whole thing was nerve-racking enough, now I had to do it with an audience in the room?

In my headphones I heard the line producer declare, thirty seconds to announce, twenty seconds to announce, ten seconds to announce, five, four, three, two, one, announce! I took off like a bat out of hell. My energy was fast. I hit every line with a clean, crisp exciting delivery. I didn't say NCAA like I feared I would. I correctly said, "NAACP Image Awards." By the time I finished the laundry list of stars appearing on the show and the introduction of the host, you would have thought I had just boxed in a twelve-round championship fight. I was sweating. I was so hyped by the moment that the only thing that brought me back to the fact I wasn't alone was the loud and robust applause from the celebrity presenter and her entourage. I couldn't believe it, they where applauding my performance. Their presence turned out to be a blessing. The challenge of not wanting to embarrass myself in front of them made me forget about my fears. In the end, I really appreciated their support.

They left the room and I continued to soar, to introduce each performer and presenter with equally deserved enthusiasm. It was magic. The show went great. The stars, the musicians, and the technical crews were fabulous. I was proud to have been part of such a classy production.

I guess the producers were happy with my work because they hired me again that spring for five episodes of their weekly television program, *Showtime at the Apollo* and their *Essence Awards* television special. Later on that summer another production company hired me to announce the *Essence Music Festival,* another television special that hailed from New Orleans. Not bad for a first-time live announcer.

VO CAREER HIGHLIGHTS

Whenever one talks about voice-over career highlights, one must consider the first job as the most precious. And so I must say that when I got on that plane for Oakland, California, to record those two Bank of America radio spots, it was the beginning of many good things to come. Landing the role of Joe Robbie Robertson on the cartoon *Spider-Man* was the next high that was soon followed by my first trailer campaign, Spike Lee's *Crooklyn*. The Alpo national television commercial felt really nice and my favorite trailer of all times *How Stella Got Her Groove Back* felt even nicer.

And then the car spots started to roll in, starting with the television campaign for the Honda Accord, to be followed by the Chevy Prism and then the Lincoln LS, to today's second-year anniversary as the voice of the Toyota Camry for television. Little did I know while growing up in Detroit and eating thousands of those tasty White Castle hamburgers that I would grow up to be the urban radio commercial spokesman for those burgers for the last four years.

Two seasons as the promo voice of *Motown Live* felt good and the two years as the promo voice of *City of Angels* on CBS felt even better. Ice Cube's *Friday* trailer was sweet and *Friday After Next* was even sweeter. E! Entertainment did me right when they chose me to narrate the *Marvin Gaye E! True Hollywood Story* segment.

We danced again when I did the *Ron "Superfly" O'Neal E! True Hollywood Story*.

From books on tape to the live announce at the *NAACP Image Awards*. From the *Essence Awards* to *Showtime at the Apollo*, I have had a great run. Today, SBC, Wells Fargo, the Hoosier Lottery, Coors, Washington Mutual, Cingular Wireless, U.S. Army, Blue Cross, Indiana Pacers, Los Angeles Clippers, Sempra Energy, and the Oregon Lottery, just to name a few, all feel great and that little black silhouette man you see on television dancing around kitchens, supermarkets, and firehouses telling us to "Jazz it up with Zatarain's" feels even better.

REVELATION

If I knew then what I know now, I might not have been so nervous that night at the *Image Awards*. It turns out that since the show would air on FOX Television a week after the live taping, any flaws that occurred could be fixed in editing. I did the *Essence Awards* and the *Essence Musical Festival* specials in postproduction—I wasn't even there the night those shows were taped. After the producers edited those shows, I went into a studio and read a final script.

Showtime at the Apollo is taped in New York, and I read those five shows from a final script in a studio in Los Angeles. The perfectionist that I am will probably always strive to not make mistakes during a taping, even though I know it can be fixed in postproduction. I also believe that if I had stunk up the joint at the amphitheatre the night of the *Image Awards*, someone else would have been used in postproduction.

In the end, the only show that truly is "live" is the Oscars because we all see it on television that very night, on both coasts, at the same time. I think the Oscar announcing job is in my immediate future—and I'll be more than ready!

This is only the beginning of your journey. I have tried to give you a road map to a successful career in the exciting and lucrative world of voice-overs. Now it's up to you to take the next step and start using your voice as a source of income.

You deserve the chance to be a winner in life so go for it! Create your own destiny and pave your own way. Remember, not everyone is going to make it in this highly competitive field, but if you are passionate about your desire and you give it your all, you'll always have the satisfaction of knowing that you tried.

For years you've heard about other people making lots of money with their voices, and for years you've said to yourself "I can do that." Now is the time for you to stop saying "I know this person who . . ." and be the person who does voice-overs!

PRAISE FOR RODNEY SAULSBERRY

"Rodney Saulsberry has one of the most magnificent voices today. The quality of his voice adds interest to any product from automotive to communications."

— Montez Miller,
Executive Talent Director, GlobalHue

"There is an honesty and believability in Rodney's voice. That's why he's been my talent for many a spot. Together we've told the virtues (and in some cases the lack thereof), for all sorts of projects . . . from burgers to banks to berating smoking cigarettes to teens. And the one thing constant in that variety of spots is Rodney's ability to cut through the clutter. You see, I write for a lot of clients, and the thing they all want from their commercials is not to just be heard, but to be listened to. And with Rod as the talent I know that won't be a problem."

—Larry Batiste,
Copywriter

"To me Rodney Saulsberry is the most talented voice-over talent I know. And what's so wonderful about Rodney is he's always willing to share his knowledge and wisdom with other aspiring voice-over talents. Before I met Rodney, I had read magazine articles about his career in Black Enterprise

and Upscale. *Today, I still refer to those articles several times a week in order to stay focused and keep my vision as I pursue my voice-over career. Rodney has revealed to me his integrity, sincerity, his desire, and his passion for what he does best. And what I admire most of all about him is he knows the source of which his talent comes from and he continues to bless others with it. I have been waiting for this book to manifest and here it is!!! And I must say it has been worth the wait. It will be highly recommended to my students because I believe in his wisdom and knowledge, and it will be my own personal handbook during my journey in this voice-over industry. Rodney I wish you much continued success and when I grow up I want to be just like you. (smile) May GOD continue to bless you from the bottom of my heart."*

—CeCe McGhee,
Voice Talent and Voice-Over Coach

Sample Copy

This appendix includes trailer, commercial, promo, narration, tag, and radio imaging copy.

NARRATION COPY

VO Direction: Magical, movie trailer-type read.

We live in a mysterious world. Our knowledge is based solely on what we see. Where crops and weeds soar like skyscrapers. Birds weigh more than boulders. Snow falls to the ground like nuclear bombs. A world where our future is not promised and our past is merely who we once were.

VO Direction: Corporate-style serious read.

Over the past several decades we have watched our economy change dramatically. The American people have come to expect and accept the ups and downs of the financial roller coaster of life. If we are to succeed in the

21st century, we must continue to be resilient and stead-fast in our pursuit of our eternal goal—complete financial independence.

VO Direction: On-hold message.

Soothe your aching muscles in the new Quatro Spa at Freemont. Enjoy our purifying facials, aromatic body wraps, and therapeutic massages. Start your incredible luxurious journey in the soothing steam rooms and listen to new age music as you meditate in the tropical rain shower rooms. You deserve this ultimate pleasure. For reservations, call extension 2-7-8-0-4.

TRAILER COPY :60 Radio Spot
FOR SWEET LOVE SWEET

VO Direction: A conversational soft sell read for this romantic comedy.

DONNY WAS ON ONE TRACK…

MICHELLE WAS ON ANOTHER.

TWO HEARTS…

ONE BEAT…

NO CLUE…

SERVO PORCHLIGHT PICTURES PRESENTS

TREY BRIGHT
SHERRY MARQUETTE
MO MONEY
NICOLA PETRI

BARRETT CANDY
AND SO DEF

SWEET LOVE SWEET

TASTE THE SUGAR ON DECEMBER 25th

TV TRAILER SPOT/ Tags

VO Direction: Read each tag three times—slow, medium, and fast.

RATED R

STARTS FRIDAY

NOW PLAYING

NOW IN SELECT CITIES. COMING TO A THEATER NEAR YOU

STARTS FRIDAY, OCTOBER 20th

STARTS FRIDAY EVERYWHERE

ADDITIONAL CITIES FRIDAY, OCTOBER 27th

COMING SOON

STARTS FRIDAY, OCTOBER 27th

RATED R . . . FOR STRONG LANGUAGE AND IMAGES OF DRUGS, VIOLENCE AND SEX

:60 RADIO COMMERCIAL SPOT

VO Direction: Non-announcery. Casual friendly read.

After every holiday it happens. You can't fit in your clothes. You walk around feeling like you're about to bust. Don't panic. If you're worried about watching your diet and counting your calories, Pinehurst is here to help with our CrushCalorie program, an easy way to identify the best foods for your low-calorie lifestyle. The next time you go to the grocery store look for our CrushCalorie signs marked clearly on foods with low calories per serving. Instantly you'll know what foods are good for your low-calorie commitment. And with plenty of tasty desserts available, Pinehurst makes the diet pleasurable, too. Rediscover your waistline and feel great about yourself again with this healthy low-calorie program from Pinehurst.

:60 RADIO COMMERCIAL

VO Direction: The surveyor—M/F (Male or Female) Be very inquisitive, kind of nerdy.

Mr. Kinsky—Middle age. Low-key, not too excited at first but warms to the idea.

ANNCR—Straight announcer read with a wink. Have fun with it. Not too serious.

SFX (Sound effects): Phone ringing then picks up

Mr. Kinsky: Hello.

SURVEY: Hello, Mr. Kinsky. I'm calling to ask you about your morning paper. Do you have a moment to talk?

Mr. Kinsky: Sure.

SURVEY: What newspaper do you read in the morning?

Mr. Kinsky: The *Daily News.*

SURVEY: What is your favorite section of the *Daily News*?

Mr. Kinsky: The sports.

SURVEY: Do you think you would like an all sports newspaper delivered to your home?

ANNC:.   When your favorite section of a newspaper is limited to giving you just a little of what you like a lot. It's time for you to consider subscribing to a paper that is dedicated solely to the subject of your interest. Introducing the *Only What You Want to Read Chronicle.*

Mr. Kinsky: I think I'd like that.

SURVEY: What part of the paper does Mrs. Kinsky like to read?

ANNCR: Our subscriptions are so affordable you can get a personal newspaper for every-one in the house.

Call 305-555-8888 or visit onlywhat youwanttoreadchronicle.org for more information on how to get this self-centered publication.

The Only What You Want to Read Chronicle—the future is now.

TV SPOT "REVIEWS"

VO DIRECTION: Bright exuberant read.

THE CRITICS HAVE SPOKEN

STRAY BULLET IS THE MOST PROVOCATIVE FILM OF THE YEAR

"A COMEDY OF SHOCKING GRAVITY, WHICH LEAVES YOU SHATTERED," HAILS ROLLING STONE

THE *NEW YORK TIMES* CALLS IT "FALL DOWN FUNNY"

AND *TIME* MAGAZINE RAVES

"IT'S SHAKESPEARE MEETS WOODY ALLEN"

"FOUR STARS"

"THE YEAR'S MOST IMPORTANT MOVIE"

STRAY BULLET

RATED R

TV PROMO TAGS

VO Direction: Read each tag three times. Fast, faster, and faster.

AT 8/7 CENTRAL, NEXT FRIDAY ON TPC

AT 8/7 CENTRAL, TPC FRIDAY

AT 8/7 CENTRAL, TONIGHT ON TPC

COMING UP NEXT ON TPC

RADIO COMMERCIAL COPY

VO Direction: Guy 1 & 2, keep it loose. Have fun. Announcer: Hip and cool. Non-announcery.

SINGERS: WE WANT TO GO. YOU WANT TO GO.
              THEY WANT TO GO. WE GOT TO GO.

SFX: DOORBELL, DOOR OPENS

GUY1:   GREAT, YOU'RE HERE.

GUY 2:   IT'S FOUR A.M. WHAT'S THE BIG
              DEAL?

GUY 1:   YOU ARE TRULY NOT GONNA
              BELIEVE THIS.

GUY 2:   BELIEVE WHAT?

GUY 1:   OVER HERE. LOOK!

GUY 2:   LOOK AT WHAT?

GUY 1:   LOOK!

GUY 2:   IT'S A CUP.

GUY1:   IT'S NOT JUST A CUP. IT'S A GLOW
              CUP WITH SHAKEY JAKE'S NEW
              LOGO ON IT!

GUY2:   AND I'M HERE BECAUSE . . .?

GUY 1:   OKAY, WATCH–NOT ME–WATCH THE
              CUP!

SFX: LIGHT SWITCH

GUY 1:   SEE?

GUY 2:   YEAH, IT'S A GLOW CUP.

GUY1:   NOW WATCH THIS.

SFX: LIGHT SWITCH

GUY1:   SEE THAT. NOW IT DOESN'T!

SFX: LIGHT SWITCH GOING OFF AND ON
              QUICKLY

GUY 1:   NOW IT GLOWS. IT DOESN'T. IT
              GLOWS. IT DOESN'T. IT GLOWS.

GUY 2:	(INTERRUPTS) YEAH, YEAH, WHAT'S YOUR POINT?
SFX:	MUSIC STOPS
GUY 1:	HOW DOES IT KNOW?
SINGERS:	WE WANT TO GO. YOU WANT TO GO. THEY WANT TO GO. WE GOT TO GO.
ANNCR:	COME IN TO SHAKEY JAKE'S AND PURCHASE A LARGE SOFT DRINK AND BE THE FIRST TO GET A FREE GLOW CUP WITH OUR NEW LOGO. GET GOIN' AND GET GLOWIN'. ONLY AT SHAKEY JAKE'S.
SINGERS:	WE WANT TO GO. YOU WANT TO GO. THEY WANT TO GO. WE GOT TO GO.
ANNCR:	SHAKEY JAKE'S. YOU HAVE TO GO!

RADIO IMAGING COPY

VO Direction: Hip radio deejay reads.

VO 1

Blazin' hip-hop and R&B. This is the fresh new sound of WINK 99. This hour, listen for your chance to win WINK 99's third fantasy getaway trip to New York to see the hip-hop show of the year! Power House 2004.

VO 2

Smooth Jazz is the way to wake up in Southern California. 92.7 the WRAP.

VO 3

Nashville's 103.5 the Party! Playing today's best new country. Kickin' off another hour of commercial-free music. Today's hot new country.

VO 4

Totally retro 99.9. It's all about the music.

Vocal Exercises

TONGUE TWISTERS

VO Direction: Here are a couple of tongue twisters for the beginning voice-over actor. Start out slow and gradually build up to a faster pace. Your goal is to read the copy as fast as you can without making a mistake and with complete clarity.

Someone said something simple
A simple something said to me
Simply simple someone said
A simple something said to me

I'm not the pretty banjo player
I'm the pretty banjo player's mate
I am only playing the pretty banjo player's banjo
'Cause the pretty banjo player's running pretty late

VO Direction: These are exercises for the more advanced voice-over actor. Beginners can start out reading them slowly until they are comfortable with faster reads.

Crooked cookies cakes and pies
Crush it crack it crapper ties
Crystal critters cry like mad
Croaking choking frogs are sad

Why in the world would a whale want water?
When a whale wants water will a well run dry?
Why in the world would a wet whale want wet water?
Will a wet whale want wet water when a wet well runs
    dry?

Taste test the tepid tea
Tea taste tepid warm to thee
Tip the waiter two times three
Two times three times four times ten
Go right back and tip again

Properly press the purple and black pleated plaid pants
    you own
Prepare to put your purple and black pleated plaid pants
    on
Properly press the purple and black pleated plaid pants
    you own
Now properly dressed in your purple and black pleated
    plaid pants be gone

BREATHING

VO Directions: Inhale deeply and repeat these words as many times as you can in one breath.

Flipping and flapping
Wishing and wanting
Dipping and dumping

Picking and popping
Fatty batty titter tatty
Sloppy floppy choppy hobby
Tick tacky tickle tackle
Super duper tricky saddle

INFLECTION

VO Directions: Change the meaning of what you say by
changing your inflection.

Say the word *sure* to imply

Enthusiasm
Definite
Sarcastic
Not sure

Say the sentence *I love spinach* to imply

You really do love it.
You despise it.
You like it just a little bit.
Sarcasm

Make the statement *I will* to indicate

Truth
Deceit
Eagerness
Maybe

DISCLAIMER

For your convenience the following resource information is provided to help you maximize your employment potential; however, I do not necessarily endorse each product and service found on these pages. If I have failed to list other companies or persons that offer the same services their omission is not intended to discredit their value.

Resources

Animation Casting

Blupka Productions
(Animation)
13223 Ventura Blvd., Ste. G
Studio City, CA 91604
818-501-1258

Donna Grillo Voice Casting
Hollywood, CA
(323) 953-2971

Ginny McSwain Voice Over
Casting
Glendale, CA 91202
(818) 548-7174

Kris Zimmerman Voice Over
Casting
San Fernando Valley, CA
(661) 259-5016

Animation Training

Bob Bergen's Animation
Voice Over Workshop
Sherman Oaks, CA
(818) 999-3081

Ginny McSwain Animation
Voice-Over Classes
Studio City, CA
(818) 548-7174

Kris Zimmerman
Burbank, CA
(661) 259-5016

Susan Blu's Workshops
Studio City, CA
(818) 509-1483

Casting Services

Carroll Voice Casting
6767 Forest Lawn Drive, #203
Los Angeles, CA 90068
(323) 851-9966

Davis/Glick
3280 Cahuenga Blvd. West
Los Angeles, CA 90068
(323) 645-2323

Elaine Craig Voice Casting
6464 Sunset Blvd., Ste. 1150
Los Angeles, CA 90028
(323) 469-8773

Kalmenson & Kalmenson
Voice Casting
5730 Wish Ave.
Encino, CA 91316
(818) 342-6499

Ken Rayzor Radioworks
1608 Argyle Ave.
Hollywood, CA 90028
(323) 466-9221

Marc Graue Voice Casting
3421 W. Burbank Blvd.
Burbank, CA 91505
(818) 953-8991

Sheila Manning Voice Casting
508 S. San Vicente Blvd.
Los Angeles, CA 90048
(323) 852-1046

The Voicecaster
1832 W. Burbank Blvd.
Burbank, CA 91506
(818) 841-5300

Voices Voicecasting
13261 Moorpark St., #102
Sherman Oaks, CA 91423
(818) 789-8460

Industry Informational Websites

LA 411.com
411 Publishing
5700 Wilshire Blvd, Ste. 120
Los Angeles, CA 90036
(323) 965-2020
www.LA411.com

LA411.com
411 Publishing
360 Park Ave. S., 17th Floor
New York, NY 10010
(646) 746-6890
www.NewYork411.com

Samuel French Inc.
7623 Sunset Blvd., Dept. W
Hollywood, CA 90046
(323) 876-0570
www.samuelfrench.com

The Great Voice Company, Inc.
616 East Palisades Avenue
Englewood Cliffs, NJ 07632
(800) 333-8108
www.greatvoice.com

Voice 123.com
The Voice-over Marketplace
www.voice123.com

Ido commercials.com
Your Commercial Depot
www.idocommercials.com

Industry Magazines

Voice-Over Resource Guide
Dave & Dave Incorporated
4352 Lankershim Boulevard
Toluca Lake, CA 91602
(818) 508-7578

Variety
5700 Wilshire Boulevard
Los Angeles, CA 90036

Adweek Magazine
770 Broadway, 7th Floor,
New York, New York 10003

Hollywood Reporter
5055 Wilshire Boulevard
Los Angeles, California 90036

Animation Magazine
30101 Agoura Court, Ste. 110
Agoura Hills, CA 91301-4301
(818) 991-2884

Backstage and Backstage West
1515 Broadway, 14th Floor
New York, NY 10035

Loop Groups

Burt Sharp
Sharp ADR Services
(818) 988-3030

Caitlin McKenna Group ADR
& Voice Casting
Pasadena, CA 91031
(626) 398-3755

Doug Stone Entertainment, Inc.
16161 Ventura Blvd. #687
Encino, CA 91436
(818) 981-3031

Loop Troop-ADR Group Voice
Casting
859 Hollywood Way #411
Burbank, CA 91505
(818) 239-1616

Recording Equipment

Telos Zephyr Express
Telos Systems
2101 Superior Avenue
Cleveland, OH 44114
(216) 241-7225
www.telos-systems.com

Sennheiser MKH 416
Sennhheiser Electronic Corp.
1 Enterprise Drive
Old Lyme, CT 06371
(877) 736-6434
www.sennheiserusa.com

Tascam CD-RH700
Teac America/Tascam
7733 Telegraph Road
Montebello, CA 90640
(323) 278-8584
www.tascam.com

Behringer Eurorack MX 802A
Behringer USA Inc.
190 West Dayton Avenue
Ste. 201
Edmonds, WA 98020
(425) 672-0816
www.behringer.com

Recording Software

Sound Forge 6.0
Sonic Foundry, Inc.
1617 Sherman Avenue
Madison, WI 53704
www.sonicfoundry.com

Musicmatch Jukebox Plus 8.1
Musicmatch, Inc.
www.musicmatch.com

Unions

American Federation of
Television and Radio Artists
(AFTRA)
Los Angeles National Office
5757 Wilshire Boulevard
Los Angeles, CA 90036
(323) 634-8100
www.aftra.org

AFTRA: New York National
Office
260 Madison Avenue
7th Floor
New York, NY 10016
(212) 532-0800
www.aftra.org

AFTRA: Chicago Office
One East Erie, Ste. 650
Chicago, IL 60611
(312) 573-8081
www.aftra.org

Screen Actors Guild (SAG)
National Office
5757 Wilshire Boulevard
Los Angeles, CA 90036
(323) 954-1600
www.sag.org

SAG: New York Office
360 Madison Avenue
12th Floor
New York, NY 10017
(212) 944-1030
www.sag.org

SAG: Chicago Office
One East Erie, Ste. 650
Chicago, IL 60611
(312) 573-8081
www.sag.org

Call the National SAG or
AFTRA office for addresses
and phone numbers of branch
offices in your area.

Training

Brian Cummings Class Act
Santa Clarita, CA
(323) 497-8900

Carroll Voice Casting
Los Angeles, CA
(323) 851-9966

The Cashman Cache of Voice
Acting Techniques
Burbank, CA
(661) 222-9300

Cindy Akers & Voicetrax West
Studio City, CA
(818) 487-9001

Delores Diehl's Voice-Over
Connection, Inc.
Hollywood, CA
(213) 384-9251

Jessica Gee Voices International
San Fernando Valley, CA
(818) 785-9185

Joyce Castellanos' Workshops
Cahuenga Pass at NOVA
Productions
(323) 969-0949

Kalmenson & Kalmenson
Voicecasting
Burbank, CA
(818) 342-6499

Lauren Adams' Voice
LA Workshops
West Hollywood, CA
(323) 953-3617

Learning Annex
11850 Wilshire Blvd., Ste. 100
Los Angeles, CA 90025
(310) 478-6677

Leigh Gilbert Voice-Over Coach
West Hollywood, CA
(323) 692-5704

Nick Omana
NOVA Productions
Los Angeles, CA
(323) 969-0949

Tina D'Marco Spanish
Workshops
Burbank, CA
(626) 458-3795

The Voicecaster
Burbank, CA
(818) 841-5300

Voices Voicecasting Workshops
Sherman Oaks, CA
(818) 789-8460

Voice Over Productions
Gerald McBride
Southfield, Mich
(248) 356-7767

Voice-Over Talent Agencies

Atlanta
Arlene Wilson Agency
(404) 876-8422

People Store
(404) 874-6448

Richard S. Hutchison
(404) 261-7824

Boston
Maggie, Inc.
(617) 536-2639

The Models Group
(617) 426-4711

Chicago
Arlene Wilson Agency
(312) 573-0200

Baker & Rowley Talent
Agency, Inc.
(312) 850-4700

Stewart Talent Management
(312) 943-3131

Dallas
The Campbell Agency
(214) 522-8991

Kim Dawson Agency
(214) 630-5161

The Mary Collins Agency
(214) 871-8900

Pastorini Bosby Talent Agency
(713) 266-4488

Denver
Donna Baldwin Talent
(303) 561-1199

Detroit
Affiliated Models Inc.
(248) 244-8770

The I Group, LLC
(248) 552-8842

The Talent Shop
(248) 644-4877

Florida
Boca Talent & Model Agency
(954) 428-4677

Coconut Grove Talent
(305) 858-3002

SunSpots Productions, Inc.
(800) 355-7768

Los Angeles
Cunningham Escott &
Dipene
(310) 475-2111

Innovative Artists
(310) 656-0400

International Creative
Management
(310) 550-4304

Sutton Barth & Vennari
(323) 938-6000

Tisherman Agency
(323) 850-6767

William Morris Agency
(310) 859-4085

Minneapolis
Moore Creative Talent, Inc.
(612) 827-3823

Nashville
Talent & Model Land
(615) 321-5596

New York
Access Talent
(212) 331-9600

Don Buchwald & Associates
(212) 867-1070

Paradigm Talent Agency
(212) 703-7540

William Morris Agency
(212) 586-5100

North Carolina
Procomm
866-438-6423

San Francisco
Look Model & Talent Agency
(415) 781-2841

The Stars Agency
(415) 421-6272

Tonry Talent Agency
(415) 543-3797

Voice Prompt Agencies

GM Voices
2001 Westside Parkway,
Suite 290
Alpharetta, GA 30004
(770) 752-4500
www.gmvoices.com

The Great Voice Company, Inc.
616 East Palisade Avenue
Englewood Cliffs, NJ 07632
(800) 333-8108
www.greatvoiceco.com

Worldly Voices, LLC
2610 Westwood Drive
Nashville, TN 37204
(615) 321-8802
www.worldlyvoices.com

AC—Adult contemporary radio format, which features light rock and pop cuts.

Actors' area—A designated space in a building for actors to wait for their chance to audition or work.

ADR—Audio Dialogue Replacement. Replacing inferior inaudible dialogue with new dialogue in a film.

Ad libs—Creative lines spoken by a voice-over actor that are not written in the copy. These made-up added lines usually come at the end of a line in the copy.

AEA—Actors Equity Association. Often called simply "Equity." This union represents stage actors.

AFTRA—American Federation of Television and Radio Artists. A union for broadcast professionals.

Agent—A talent representative who seeks employment and negotiates contracts.

Animation—The creation of artificial moving images. Cartoons.

Audition—A tryout; a hearing to try out an actor or singer for a commercial, etc.

Audiobook—A reading of a book by a voice-over artist on tape.

Avail—A performer's availability to work on a certain job. Avails have no legal or contractual status.

Bio—Short for "biography." A résumé in narrative form, usually for a printed program or press release.

Booking—When a voice-over actor is officially hired for a job.

Boutique agency—A prestigious small talent agency that intentionally represents a small group of voice-over actors.

Bumper—A prerecorded audio element that acts as a transition to or from a program.

Buyout—A one-time fee for your services. No residuals. Non-union.

Callback—Follow-up interview or audition.

Casting Director—A representative responsible for choosing performers for consideration by the producer or director.

CD-ROM—Compact Disc Read Only Memory. A data storage medium. Popular for the distribution of large databases and of software, especially multimedia applications.

CHR—Contemporary Hit Radio (formerly top forty) radio format.

Class A usage—Maximum national network usage of a television commercial. Top pay.

Cold read—Reading copy out loud in an audition or performance for the first time without the benefit of a rehearsal or practice.

Control room—An area in a studio that houses all of the recording equipment.

Copy—The text of a commercial. The script.

Cross fade—A technique in which the engineer mixes sound between two sources by fading one down while at the same time raising the volume of the second source. As one becomes prominent the other is faded entirely.

Dat—Digital Audio Tape. The highest quality of recording tape.

Demo—A recorded one-and-a-half- to two-minute sample of voice-over spots to demonstrate the talent of the performer.

Dialogue—The words in the ad copy.

Diaphragm—A large mass of muscle that separates the thoracic cavity from the abdominal cavity; one of the main muscles that support the voice.

Documentary—A nonfiction video or film that depicts actual events using real people not actors.

Double—A commercial spot featuring two characters.

Double scale—Getting paid two times the scale rate for a voice-over job.

Dry voice-over commercials—Commercials that consist of voices only, no music beds.

Dub—A copy of a piece of audio.

Dubbing—Dialogue replacement in a foreign film.

Edit notes—Written instruction the engineer uses to fix mistakes in a recording session.

Enunciate—To pronounce and announce clearly; to state definitely.

EPK—Electronic Press Kit. A video presentation with a voice-over narration, interviews from the actors and director promoting the making of a movie.

ETA—Estimated Time of Arrival.

Ethnic—To sound like a particular group of people. Imitate their language characteristics.

Final—The completed approved version of a produced movie trailer.

FTP—File Transfer Protocol. A client server protocol that allows a user on one computer to transfer files to and from another computer over a network.

Hard sell—Read the copy with an aggressive delivery.

Holding fee—A voice actor receives a check from a production company to hold a commercial she worked on for a later airdate.

House reel—The agency demo tape that features samples of their talent roster.

ID—The station's call letters. For example, a signature voice artist working for a jazz station with the call letters, WJZZ might say "You're listening to smooth jazz on WJZZ."

Improvs—Short for "improvisation." The actor creates dialogue based on a given theme or premise.

Infomercial—A long commercial that gives you information on a particular product.

In-store—An audio/visual commercial that plays exclusively inside a store near the product it is promoting.

Interstitials—Short vignettes in radio and television that play between the core programming.

ISDN—International Standard Digital Network or Integrated Services Digital Network. A device used to record a voice-over session through digital telephone lines.

Iso booth—A soundproof isolation room within the recording studio where the voice-over artist records.

Level—A vocal sample of the volume level that you plan to speak given to the engineer during a session.

Liners—One-line dry voice-over (no music) reads for a radio station.

Live announce—The broadcast live from a venue in real time without edit.

Loop group—A group of actors that provide background sound effects for TV and film in postproduction.

Looping—See "ADR."

M/F—Male/Female. This abbreviation is used as a character description in a script indicating the role in question can be played by a man or woman.

Mic—Microphone.

MP3 file—A compressed audio format that reduces the size of a sound file without hurting the quality of the sound.

Music bed—A musical accompaniment that plays underneath a voice-over in a commercial.

NAB—National Association of Broadcasters. A trade group for radio and television license holders.

Narration—Assimilating information and retelling it; the art of storytelling.

Off-mic—Speaking to the side of the microphone. Not directly in the center or diaphragm. Off-axis.

Phone patch—A director directs session on the telephone from another location.

Pick-up session—A session for re-recording lines that were not perfect in the first session.

Plosives—Words that begin with P, T, or B.

Popping—A burst of air that comes from your mouth that distorts and overloads the microphone.

Postproduction—The finishing touches applied to a commercial after the talent is done.

Program director—The person who controls the on-air functions of a radio station; the format, programming, and everything a listener hears over the air.

Promo—A recorded announcement promoting a production on television and radio.

PSA—Public Service Announcement.

Radio imaging—A "station voice" who does all of the IDs, promos, liners, and sweepers that represent the station's image.

Residuals—Monies received by performers for replays of their work on television and radio.

Reuse—A fee paid to the talent for the rerun of a commercial. A new cycle.

Run-through—Rehearsing a show or rehearsing some copy before recording it.

Safety—Redoing a good take exactly the same way just in case there was some technical problem with the first take.

SAG—Screen Actors Guild; this union represents television and motion picture performers.

S.A.S.E.—Self-Addressed Stamped Envelope.

Scale—The union base wage for an actor for a recording session.

Scale plus ten—Union base wage plus ten percent for your agent's ten percent commission; the ten percent does not come out of your base pay.

Scratch track—The unfinished version of a commercial that you have to watch or listen to before you add your professional voice to the final spot.

Sennheiser—Voice-over industry standard directional microphone.

Sessions—The period of time in the studio where voice-over talent records the copy for the commercial, promo, trailer etc.

SFX—This stands for "sound effects."

Signature voice—The talent who does all of the commercials for a certain product.

Slate—You say your name before a take in an audition. In a session the engineer will say (slate) the number of each take before recording.

Smile—A technique used to warm up and brighten your copy delivery.

SOT—Sound On Tape.

Soft sell—Read the copy with a more laid-back approach.

Sound check—Before a session, the engineer makes sure that each actor is audible when speaking into a microphone.

Sound Forge 6.0—A voice-over editing software created by Sonic Foundry.

Sony Professionals—Voice-over industry standard headphones.

Spec—Short for "speculative." A non-air demo commercial is recorded with the intention to possibly air in the future.

Sweepers—Fully produced Station IDs with music beds.

Tags—Short lines that end a spot.

Takes—Every time you start to record in a recording session it is called a "take." Example, the first time you record a commercial spot is take 1, the second time is take 2, etc. If you make a mistake and have to start over, it is considered another take.

Talkback Box—An audio communications tool for various locations to talk with one another to coordinate events. Primarily used by the director, announcer, and all ancillary staff. Always switched on so everything the director says is heard at all times. The announcer also uses the talkback box to open his microphone so the audience can hear him during a live broadcast.

Telos Zephyr Express—A portable ISDN digital audio transceiver/mixer

Tempo—The speed in which you speak. Slowly or quickly.

Tongue twisters—A group of words or sentences that require a concentrated effort to enunciate; used as vocal warm-ups or exercises.

Trailer—A vocal narration underneath clips promoting an upcoming film.

Urban—A sound that represents the vocal characteristics of minorities in a certain city.

Vanity plates—Personalized license plates.

Vendor—A movie trailer production house.

VO—Voice-over; an off-camera voice coming from an actor not in the frame.

Voice-over—Anything that has to do with vocal representation via media.

Warm up the copy—Make the copy friendly and more intimate.

BIBLIOGRAPHY

Alburger, James. *The Art of Voice Acting: The Craft and Business of Performing for Voice-over*. Woburn, MA: Focal Press, 1998.

Apple, Terri and Gary Owens. *Making Money in Voice-Overs: Winning Strategies to a Successful Career in Commercials, Cartoons and Radio*. Los Angeles: Long Eagle Publishing, 1999.

Barzman, Alan. *Hearing Voices: Creating, Voicing & Producing Great Radio Commercials*. Sherman Oaks, CA: Gabriel Publications, 2003.

Blue, Susan and Molly Ann Mullin. *Word of Mouth: A Guide to Commercial and Animation Voice-over Excellence*. Beverly Hills: Pomegranate Press Ltd., 1996.

Clark, Elaine A. *There's Money Where Your Mouth Is: An Insider's Guide to a Career in Voice-overs* New York: Backstage Books, 1995.

Hogan, Harlan. *VO: Tales and Techniques of a Voice-Over Actor.* New York: Allworth Press, 2002.

Thomas, Sandy. *So You Want to Be a Voice-over Star.* Wantagh, NY: In the Clubhouse Publishing, 1999.

HOW TO CONTACT THE AUTHOR

Agency Representation:

William Morris Agency
151 El Camino Drive
Beverly Hills, CA 90212
(310) 859-4289
www.wma.com

Tomdor Publishing
P.O. Box 1735
Agoura Hills, CA 91376-1735
(818) 207-2682
www.tomdorpublishing.com

Web Contact:

E-mail:
rodtalks@rodneysaulsberry.com or
rodtalks@aol.com

Website:
www.rodneysaulsberry.com or
www.a1voice.com

ORDER FORM

PLEASE SEND ME THE FOLLOWING

_____ copies of *You Can Bank on Your Voice: Your Guide to a Successful Career in Voice-Overs* ISBN 0-9747678-0-8 $16.95 each copy.

Please copy, fill out, mail, fax, or go online

Name: _____

Address: _____

City, State, Zip:_____

Telephone: _____

E-mail address:_____

Fax this form to: 818-707-8591

Website Orders: www.tomdorpublishing.com

Postal Orders: Make check or money order payable to: Tomdor Publishing, P.O. Box 1735, Agoura Hills, CA 91376-1735; Telephone: 818-207-2682

Sales Tax: Add 8.25% to orders delivered in California.

Shipping and Handling: $4.00 per book

Total amount enclosed $ _____

Charge to my MC/ Visa / AMEX
Card # _____

Signature as on the card _____
Exp. Date _____